# OFF THE PAGE

*Writers Talk About Beginnings, Endings,*

*and Everything In Between*

EDITED BY

# CAROLE BURNS

INTRODUCTION BY MARIE ARANA

W. W. NORTON & COMPANY

*New York · London*

For information about special discounts for bulk purchases,
please contact W. W. Norton Special Sales at
specialsales@wwnorton.com or 800-233-4830.

Manufacturing by Victor Graphics
Book design by JAM Design
Production manager: Devon Zahn

Library of Congress Cataloging-in-Publication Data

Off the page : writers talk about beginnings, endings, and everything
in between / edited by Carole Burns. — 1st ed.
p. cm.
ISBN 978-0-393-33088-5 (pbk.)
1. Authors, American—20th century—Interviews.
2. Authors, English—20th century—Interviews.
3. Fiction—Authorship.  I. Burns, Carole, 1964–
PS129.O45 2008
810.9'005—dc22
                                                    2007029971


W. W. Norton & Company, Inc.
500 Fifth Avenue, New York, N.Y. 10110
www.wwnorton.com

W. W. Norton & Company Ltd.
Castle House, 75/76 Wells Street, London W1T 3QT

1 2 3 4 5 6 7 8 9 0

# OFF THE PAGE

*For Ace and Dee*

# Contents

# Preface

In every one of my interviews with writers for washington post.com's "Off the Page," *The Washington Post*'s online literary chat show, there was a moment when I knew I was hearing something extraordinary—for its intelligence, for its insight into literature and writing, for a freshness that made me suspect that the writer had not said it exactly this way before. With Martin Amis, it was his quick riposte to a question about his critics, particularly harsh in Britain: "I am now seen as a drawling Oxonian, and a genetic elitist, who took over the family firm. I'm not a toff. I'm a yob." With A. S. Byatt, it was the revelation that she begins her novels not with words in mind, not with ideas, but with colors. With Richard Bausch, it was his passionate response to a reader doubting whether writing can be taught. "I don't teach writing," he growled back. "I teach patience. Toughness. Stubbornness. The willingness to fail. I teach the life."

I would hear these words and know that I was committing them to memory so I could tell my father, an inveterate reader, as if relaying to him the latest gossip from the neighborhood; so I could pass on this bit of wisdom about character or place to the university students to whom I teach writing and literature; and so I could apply this knowledge to writing my own novel.

At some point, I realized that in these interviews, the authors were touching on all the vital elements of fiction and writing: the initial glimmer of an idea, how a writer shapes and changes that idea, how characters come to life, playing with language and style, the struggles of the writing life, its joys. This wasn't just a series of journalistic interviews anymore. It was a rich store of information and ideas about writing and literature that could be shaped into a book.

Here is that book. By now, I have conducted forty-one "Off the Page" interviews on washingtonpost.com with forty-three different authors, ranging from Pulitzer Prize winners such as Edward P. Jones and Richard Ford to first-time writers such as Hannah Tinti and Doreen Baingana. I've arranged the material into chapters—first a section that guides readers through the writing process, then a section on the writing life—trying to make order of the fertile chaos. But the best way to read this book may be out of order: Open any page and see what you find.

I began conducting these interviews in October 2003, when I was a news editor at *The Washington Post*'s Web site. As host, I would book the authors, write an introduction about their work, and then interview them, asking my own questions as well as working in queries from the online audience at washingtonpost.com. What always struck me about the interviews was how much the authors seemed to enjoy them. Stilted at first, writers warmed quickly to the format as they kept encountering questions that reflected a serious interest in writing and literature. During a reading or in a print interview, sometimes you can tell that a writer has heard a question countless times and is providing the same answer that he or she has given countless times. With "Off the Page," the combination of the freewheeling nature of the online world and the serious tone of the questions both loosened up authors and gave them the time and inclination to provide thoughtful answers.

The online interview format is casual indeed. It is less formal than a bookstore reading or even a magazine interview, with one rather serious journalist interviewing the author. Usually, writers talked to me over the phone while at home or in a hotel room in the midst of a book tour. (At first, I was at the washingtonpost.com offices, but then, after moving to England, I talked to them from my own home or, twice, from a university classroom with students watching.) I would read a question from me or a member of our online audience (writing in from places such as Washington; New York; Lenexa, Kansas; Kassel, Germany). The writer would dictate an answer while I frantically typed, then I'd send it out live.

Our eclectic online audience helped make the interviews lively. The online regulars of "Off the Page" are a well-read bunch whose queries often impressed the award-winning writers answering them. "This is a very astute question," I can still hear Joyce Carol Oates saying in her quiet, measured voice when someone asked her if writers had a "quarrel with reality." On another show, the British writer Tim Parks was asked about Hellas's prospects in European football that autumn. Not all of these people hang out at a bookstore on Saturday night.

The chatty nature of the exchange also allowed the quirky to occur. Richard Bausch admitted that he was speaking from a parking garage at Dulles Airport because he couldn't find his car. "Can I say that?" I asked. "Go ahead," he said. Shortly after the show finished, Bausch was offered a ride home.

As I reread the chapters now, there are times the conversation takes on the tone of a dinner party with a couple of Pulitzer Prize winners and your favorite mystery writer, when the fourth bottle of wine is being opened and everyone is beginning to relax. It's entertaining. It's a little gossipy. It's fun.

And then I read more deeply. I slow down and take in the complexity of each quote, the evidence of years' worth of hard-won knowledge about fiction, the seriousness with which every writer included in this book takes the business of his or her craft. It's a lot more than repartee. Theirs is a rich and varied dialogue about writing and literature. Although I usually interviewed just one author on each show, it sometimes feels as if the writers are talking back and forth, exchanging ideas, sharpening an answer in response to another writer's thoughts. And of course, as writers, they not only know what to say about writing—they also know how to say it. They are practiced with words. Michael Cunningham inspires, A. S. Byatt is erudite, Tod Goldberg is funny, Stuart Dybek riffs. They all find the right words.

Sometimes, their answers can sound like variations on a theme. The thoughts of these very different writers on voice or endings are the same, and different, at once. In the chapter on character, "Haven't I Seen You Somewhere Before?" Russell Banks echoes E. L. Doctorow as he talks about using historical figures as characters in a novel, and Colm Tóibín has a slightly different twist on how he drew Henry James for his novel *The Master,* and then Marie Arana talks about how the protagonist in her novel is her father, her husband, herself, and a new personality altogether, which fits in with

Jhumpa Lahiri's calling her characters inventions of the many people she's known, which is similar to Marisha Pessl's ideas about using strangers she sees on the street as models (she can "invent their histories, their joys and sorrows"), which is of course a version of what Russell Banks did when he imagined Owen Brown of *Cloudsplitter*—he is and isn't Owen Brown—which is only a few steps away from Richard Ford's blunt declaration about the narrator of his major novels: "Frank Bascombe's not anybody." We travel a long distance in that chapter, but it is not a straight line—more like interlocking spirals. Each writer takes us on his own distinct journey, yet they swerve in and around similar ideas, and they do so in every chapter in this book.

Nor do the quotes fit neatly into one chapter or another. As I was putting this book together, I pinned every quote on the wall of my studio, in vertical columns by chapter, so I could easily rearrange them within the chapters and see them all at once. (Friends visiting called it "installation art"—I plan to do this with my novel soon, if only so it looks as if there's a physical object I'm working on.) As I rearranged the chapter on theme, I'd find a quote that wasn't quite fitting and try it out in "All That Jazz." And then back again. And then I'd try it out in "Musing About the Muse." Parsing the writing process into topics is simply not clear-cut—it can't be diagrammed like a sentence. Each part bleeds into the next. And the next. And the next.

This idea—of the interconnectedness of a whole—moves me. My partner, who's a painter, talks about how when you change one color in a painting, all the other colors look different. (No, he's just told me. They *are* different.) Somehow it seems related to living, to existing on earth. It's Christmas, and I'm reminded of the core message of *It's a Wonderful*

*Life*—every life affects so many others. And so it is with fiction. Character is place is theme is voice is style. All of these
elements join up. All of them—even the tiniest word or
sentence—contribute to the whole.

Of course, this only makes writing all the more difficult.
Which is why readers begin asking writers questions about
how they started, how they do it. Paper? Computer?
Ballpoint or fountain pen? Please give us a clue! And there is
something mysterious about the process of creating art after
all. Writers do not know the answer to every question about
how a piece of writing came into being. There are moments
they can trace—such as the first time Walter Mosley heard
Easy Rawlins speak to him—but at other times, something
happens that is impossible to understand: Writers create work
greater than themselves.

These are some of the mysteries this book explores. The
chapters are made up of anecdotes, advice, rants, pleas, digres-
sions, confessions, impressions. The writers are smart, funny,
self-deprecating, confident, questioning, elegiac, blunt. What
strikes me most of all is how every one makes such an honest attempt at giving the clearest answers possible to questions
on complex topics that could not be closer to their hearts. I
think of Stuart Dybek when he talks about Miles Davis's
*Kind of Blue* in "All That Jazz"; Alice McDermott in "Truth
or Dare?" when she calls fiction the place one finds "the eternal truths"; Michael Cunningham in "Words of Wisdom,"
urging his students toward "ambitious failure"; Richard Ford
in "The Writing Life," talking about buying a new notebook
because writing is what he's "on the earth to do."

I could go on and on. But I don't have to. It's all right here.

—CAROLE BURNS

# Introduction

## by Marie Arana

The hard part, Tom Stoppard famously wrote, is getting to the top of page one. But if starting a book is hard, sustaining the pace is harder still, and following through is downright Sisyphean. So let's say it right here at the very beginning of this eye-opening collection of writerly confessions: Good writing is difficult—so difficult that writers, having lived through the agonies of purgatory, deserve to climb straight to heaven. Just take a sheet of paper, the dramatist Gene Fowler once counseled, put it in the typewriter, and bleed. You get the idea. There is nothing easy about the literary life. It's a punishing profession. Sissies need not apply.

And yet, like the most compelling of musical or ballet performances—like all good art—good writing looks so effortless, a reader can be fooled into thinking he can do it himself. "You've written a novel?" a man at a cocktail party once said to me. "I'd write one, too, if only I had the spare time!" It doesn't help that much of what gets published today is writing that is done too quickly, with too little thought, and an eye to easy commerce.

The simple truth, as any seasoned writer knows, is that there is no magic formula, no set way to write a book. You cannot be taught how to be a novelist. There is no manual, no clear curriculum. But the marvelous corollary to that simple truth is that every writer forges a private way, sets personal rules, fashions an individual technique. A writer learns to pursue the craft as he or she will. One may prefer to write by hand (I do); one may need to write the last sentence first (as John Irving so famously does); or draw the characters' faces in living color (as Gail Godwin once confessed she needs to do); or take little breaks by doing high kicks by the river (Esmeralda Santiago). But the lesson of this remarkable book is that each writer here finds a separate way. Seeing the thrilling variety of approaches laid out in these interviews can only give a new writer heart.

After more than a quarter-century in books—first as a book editor in two publishing houses, then as editor of the *Washington Post's Book World*, and, most recently, as the author of a handful of books—I've developed my own theory of what it takes to become a writer, what predisposes someone to the difficult task. First, I'm convinced it helps to be an outsider, a person who doesn't quite fit—an oddball. Having that skew on the world gives you a third eye somehow, the ability to see stories in every person you encounter, every window you glance through. I had the great, good fortune to be born of a Peruvian father and an American mother. I didn't know it at the time, absorbed as I was by my two-headed circus act, living a life fraught with anxieties and alienation, but that gnawing realization that I was rent between two countries turned out to be my greatest gift. There is nothing like trouble to get you writing.

Second, and I'm really quite serious about this: It helps to have a split personality. For, as you will read in every one of these testimonials, a writer needs to wear two hats. On the one hand, you need to be the child, the fool, a person who is willing to take risks and reveal your soul. On the other hand, you need to be your most ruthless critic, the harridan with the red pen who goes over that miserable stew of a first draft and rewrites it again and again until something of worth emerges. A good writer, in other words, must be frank-hearted, but mean as a tick.

Coming as I did from the mean side of the equation—the editorial side—I was well into middle age before I ginned up the courage to write a book. Writing is not what an editor is supposed to do. Working in book editing circles is much like living in a monastic order. A book editor opines, considers the mechanisms of an author's technique, says what needs to be done, much in the way a priest opines on a marriage, worries about the children, counsels parents on the best way to raise them. But a priest doesn't marry or have children himself; and a book editor doesn't sit down to write books. Suffice it to say that, when I first began to write, I felt unmoored. The critical faculty I had honed for so long didn't serve me at all. I needed to let go, stop wondering at every turn what the editor in me would do. I needed to surrender to the messy business of invention. And then, at the end of each day, when I'd finally produced my meager quota of eight hundred words, I would put them away, grateful that the red-penned harridan in me would slap them into shape in the morning.

Perhaps it was merciful that I began with nonfiction. I had it in mind many years ago to write a history of rubber tapping in Peru at the turn of the nineteenth century, when the automotive industry was at the cusp of efflorescence: a boring subject, you might think. But that systematic raid of the Amazon rainforest struck me as an important crossroad in environmental history. I had been drawn to the story by a figure in my own family, a distant cousin of my great-grandfather who was a rubber magnate and possibly one of the richest men of his time. His name eventually became so linked to human rights abuses, so smeared in the courts of international scandal, that my family decided to cut off all kindred ties. We were taught to say we were not related to him. In time, it was that family lie that most interested me, and it became the germ of my family memoir, *American Chica*, which ultimately is about the challenges of bicultural life and the deep, seismic scissures between North and South America. It was not an easy book to write. But working in nonfiction is like breaking rock, finding a shape in the information, polishing reality to a high shine. The material is ever there, absolute and irrefutable.

Working in fiction, I quickly learned when I sat down to write my novel *Cellophane*, was something else altogether. The novel started with a mere feeling—the most fleeting of sensations. I had fallen in love and felt utterly transparent, as if I were wrapped in diaphanous film. I wrote the word "cellophane" on a piece of paper. That was how it began. Pure air. There was no rock. No irrefutable fact, save all the research I struggled to plumb every day in order to feel anchored, to make each character seem more real. Summoning the unreal was the hard part—excruciating for an editor whose lifework is to fiddle with other people's writing. But little by little, as

I pushed away the nitpicking editor and brought on the day-dreaming fool, as I pulled characters out of sheer air and let them have their way with me, the novel began to grow. Somehow. It was, as I say, the most grueling work I've ever done in my life. And yet the most exhilarating. You see what I mean about split personalities.

But there's more to a novelist's Jekyll and Hyde. For all the solitude and discipline the profession requires—for all the months and years you will spend as a recluse and introvert—at the finish, when your novel is finally published, you will be expected to molt into the most dynamic of extroverts. Imagine the transformation: You begin as a mad scientist in pajamas, ransacking the house for cogs and gears, making sure miters and joints fit, polishing your contraption manically . . . and then you end up trying to figure out what jacket to wear to face your readers, wondering how in God's name to *talk* about your writing, forcing yourself into the soul of sociability and grace.

It is so bizarre a career that there is nothing more reassuring than knowing how others get through it. How do they discipline themselves? Do they write into the wee hours of morning as Dostoyevsky was said to do? Or do they sit down in the morning with a good pot of café-con-leche, a la García Marquéz, and work until the church bells chime three? Do they chisel the words they produce every day? Or do they wait to edit until they have a full chapter? Do they outline a plot and stick to it? Or do they go with the flow and leave it to characters' whims? Do they truly invent every detail they write, as Anne Tyler once claimed to have done? Or do they steal promiscuously from friends and family, as I readily confess I do? Do they stick to a place they know, as Orhan Pamuk did in *Snow*? Or do they invent their own Yoknapatawpha?

Maybe they write about places they don't know at all, as John Updike did in *Brazil* or Martin Cruz Smith in *Gorky Park*.

I confess I am fascinated by the myriad ways a writer can be a writer. It is the true lesson a good education in books can convey. Creative writing schools can go only so far in teaching you how to construct a good paragraph, winnow your sentences to hard muscle. What you really end up learning in a writing community is the million little ways writers get things done.

This then is what this book ultimately offers: a community of like-minded people, willing to talk about quirks of technique, sources of inspiration, life ambitions, the darkest of writerly fears. What is truly valuable here is the interactive spirit of Carole Burns's encounters, her bubbling conversations by the fire. Writers are made to feel at home—they are responding, after all, in the written word. And perhaps because they are in the comfort of their own homes, tapping out answers on the very keyboards that hold all their secrets, they respond with a rare candor. But let's give credit where it's due: the questions posed by our online host are deeply interesting. Burns has done her homework; and the participants who step forward to prod forward the themes provide a welcome freshness. What emerges, then, is a marvelously diverse mosaic of the radically different ways writers see their own work.

I felt that special intimacy in an interview with Burns just after the publication of *Cellophane*. As any writer knows, it's not easy to talk about the process of creating a book. Oh sure, I'd drummed up a few stories of how I had researched the tribes and botany of the Amazon jungle, or how my hero was a conflation of an audacious great uncle and my brilliant father. I had created a little spiel on how the idea of the book first came into my head. But the truth is that writing, like reading (or dying, for that matter), is a private act—faced alone—impossible to chat about in easy conversation, and so the feeling I had as I was typing out answers to Burns's probing and sympathetic questions, was how different this was from standing at a podium. How candid I could be. It was a comfortable, seductive medium. I ended up babbling about events in my own life, which of course were the impetus for the whole story.

That is the secret behind this book. In that seemingly private space, in that comfortable digital womb, a writer tends to say what is on her mind, offer up the most intimate reflections. From A. S. Byatt's rich, opening cameo of how she sees her novels in colors, to Joyce Carol Oates's final little sting about the difference between a professional and an amateur, this is a surprisingly revealing collection—an intimate glimpse into lives off the page. For all who already know that writing is hard, filled with equal portions of desperation and joy, this will come as a cheering testament. And for all who are called to write—who have absolutely no choice in the matter—here is your wise companion.

WASHINGTON, DC
APRIL 2007

# OFF THE PAGE

# In the Beginning Was . . .

## *(A) The Word, (B) A Bunch of Words, (C) Not a Single Damned Word*

*L**ast night I dreamt I went to Manderley again.*
*Mrs. Dalloway said she would buy the flowers herself.*
*Call me Ishmael.*

Begin at the beginning. If only it were that easy! To pen a fitting and memorable first line, to expand naturally into a first paragraph that sets up the characters and story without giving too much away, to keep writing until one has completed a first chapter that sends the reader plunging into the next, and the next . . .

Few writers begin at the beginning, but how they find their way to a first idea, how that first glimmer turns into a novel, is itself a story. Some start with characters, some start with story, some start with an image in their head. In one of the most vivid revelations in this book, A. S. Byatt admits that her complex, intellectual fiction takes shape in her mind as blocks of color. Tim Parks finds that he can have an idea for years, until another story comes along and intersects it—and he's begun. Joanna Scott follows a lot of dead ends until something clicks. Edward P. Jones thought about his Pulitzer Prize–winning *The Known World* for about ten years before he wrote much of it down.

Richard Bausch believes that writing, when he's beginning a new piece, takes an animal instinct. You must not overthink it. You must rely on the gut.

Which is what Stuart Dybek says about endings.

But for now, the beginning.

## A. S. BYATT

I see my writing as blocks of color before it forms itself. The Frederica Quartet is easy to describe. *The Virgin in the Garden* was red, white, and green, and the red was blood and the white was stone and the green was grass. *Still Life* started out very dark purple, and then I felt there ought to be yellow—it was the complementary color to the purple. And because I felt there ought to be yellow, I thought of van Gogh's chair, and in fact van Gogh became an important symbolic figure in that book. He got in because of the color yellow.

*Babel Tower* is black and red, because of blood and destruction. And *A Whistling Woman* is quite difficult, because it tries to tie them all together. In fact, it combines the colors of all the others. At the end there are two scenes of fire. One is a real fire when the students burn down the university, and the second is a metaphorical fire when Frederica is looking over the moors and all the gorse is in bloom, and as far as you can see it looks as though the land is on fire, but it's only flowers. And the colors of *A Whistling Woman* are the *Babel Tower* colors, which are the real fire, and the *Still Life* yellow, which is the harmless fire.

I think it's the way my brain makes order, which is why I'm interested in order in Matisse.

## MICHAEL CUNNINGHAM

I always start with a character and can't really imagine doing it any other way. A character of course implies emotions and situations and conflicts and you go on from there. One of the things I learned from Virginia Woolf is that every day in everybody's life contains just about everything we need to know about human life, more or less the way the single strand of DNA contains the blueprint for the entire organism. And I believe that if we look carefully enough at anybody, and look with enough compassion and discernment, and bring to that person a certain merciless clarity, we have a novel by definition. I never think in terms of message. I don't know anything my readers don't know. I have no wisdom to pass along to them.

## MARIE ARANA

It was a feeling first.

I had fallen in love and felt emotionally naked. So there was that issue of transparency. I felt people could see through me and into my heart.

Of course they couldn't.

And then I began to think a lot about what they could see. Which brought me to the issues of truth.

*Cellophane* was my title before I realized I would be writing about paper. And being a paper engineer's daughter, I knew a lot about paper factories.

It sounds, I know, as if I backed into the story. But that's how it happened, I swear.

## RICHARD BAUSCH

I start writing with an image or a voice, but I don't know anything when I start. The only thing I know is that I'm starting. And I learn it as I go. That's why it's so hard, you have to learn all over again, because each one is different. I've written sixteen books, and I had to learn how to write each one of them. The real artistry comes with rewriting. And that's where the real work is. But at no time is it a rational thing that I'm doing. It's at the level of an animal smelling blood. It's that kind of knowledge. And if it does not surprise me, I don't trust it.

When you're dreaming it up the first time, you are using the side of you that looks out your eyes when you wake up from a nightmare and for an instant don't remember what species you are. That's the part of you you're dreaming it out of. Then when you've dreamed it up, you go through it again and again and again, using more and more the side of you that figures out how to open up the gate when you've got two bags of groceries in your arms and you don't want to put them down. And that's really all there is to it. It's simple in the same way that virtue is simple, which means, it's damned near impossible to do.

## TOD GOLDBERG

How I get started is pretty simple, really. A word, or an image, or an emotion will come to me, along with a person who feels it, and then a world sort of develops in my mind: Who would feel this? Why would they feel it? What kind of person is dealt this particular consequence? Next thing I know, I've got a big mug-o'-coffee, sad music on the stereo, I'm dressed in all black and typing.

## PAUL AUSTER

It's always the story. The story first and last. And the stories come to me out of my unconscious. I never look for them. They find me. And I'm not consciously writing about so-called ideas, but the thoughts and ideas of the characters become crucial to the telling of the story. Sometimes you start with something, and then the more you explore it, the more ramifications you discover in the image or the events. But I rarely know exactly what I'm doing. I don't work from a prearranged outline. I have a general sense of the shape of the story, who the characters are, and a sense of the beginning, the middle, and the end.

And yet once I start to write, things begin to change quite rapidly, and I've never written a book that ended up the way I thought it would be when I started. For me, I find the book in the process of writing it. Which makes it a great adventure. If it's all mapped out in advance, there's nothing to discover. It's happened to me that I've thought of stories so much and for such a long time that by the time I sit down to try to write them, they're already dead, and I feel that I don't want to write them, because I know them too well. It's the not knowing that makes it exciting.

## GISH JEN

It's not like you have one flash and the whole story appears. But I had some "amiable irritants"—you know that Philip

Roth term? He says that every writer needs "amiable irritants." I think he means we need certain things that provoke
us into action. Because, let's face it, writing a book is a lot of
work and nothing holds you to the keyboard like irritation.


## E. L. DOCTOROW

Many of my stories and books come out of an image in my
mind that I find evocative without knowing quite what it
means, so I write the story to find out. With "Child, Dead, in
the Rose Garden," from *Sweet Land Stories*, the image was of
a small body wrapped in a white shroud with a little Nike
sneaker peeking out. And then apparently I realized it was in
the Rose Garden. And that's how the story came to be.


## DAN CHAON

With *You Remind Me of Me*, there were actually several pieces
that I was working on at once. One had to do with a young
man who had been scarred by a dog. That came from a
Cleveland news story about a kid who had been scarred by a
dog, and I was fascinated not only by the attack itself but by
the prospect of having these very noticeable facial scars that
would be the first thing people noticed when they met you.

The other piece that I had was this guy, Troy, who was a
small-time drug dealer. I was particularly taken by his character, by this smart but uneducated working-class guy who
had a close relationship with his son. I was working on a story
about him but I didn't have a plot to go with it. So as I began
working on these things, I began to see how they fit together,
and how they worked in a novelistic way rather than a short-
story way.

## ANTHONY DOERR

I often take notes before I start writing. With *About Grace*, I remember I was at my parents' house in Cleveland and I had the book *Snow Crystals*, by Wilson Bentley, containing 2,500 images of snow crystals. He was one of the first people to put a camera on top of a microscope, and he took pictures of snowflakes for about fifty years. Often, people buy the book for children, just image after image of snowflakes. It's so remarkable. I kept reading about how he took these pictures. You have to capture them on a piece of black felt, and if it's way too windy, all the crystals break anyway. Then you have to transfer it to a glass slide. He'd work outside with mittens on, build a little shed to work in, and then the lamp from the microscope had heat, and there'd be that hurdle to overcome as well. So anyway, he never made any money—the book was published after his death, after he died of pneumonia, taking photos. So just that dedication to beauty, to curiosity, to that inquiry, just interested me. I was so interested in that, and I shared that with him—I wanted to give a character that attribute. My main character in *About Grace*, David Winkler, ends up having this book. So in some ways, Winkler started with that.

## ELIZABETH GRAVER

I always clip articles out of newspapers and magazines that interest me. I dump them into a big box, and often they just sit there, get covered by other stuff, come to nothing.

My novel *Awake*, for example, was probably started in 1990. I read a cover story in *People* magazine called "Children of the Dark," about kids with a very rare genetic disease called xeroderma pigmentosum (or XP), which means they have a flawed DNA repair system and cannot be exposed to daylight without a huge risk of skin cancer. The subject intrigued me. I saved the article. But it wasn't until 1999 that it somehow surfaced again.

I can't say why exactly, except that I was at a stage in my life where I was thinking about having a baby and mulling over all the questions of safety and danger, identity and love, sacrifice and connection, that parenting brings up. The article was the seed for the book. I then did quite a lot of research and also, of course, invented a great deal, focusing primarily on the identity of Anna, the mother of a child with XP, and what happens to her when she goes with her family to a camp for kids with the disease. I was drawn to the idea of a world turned upside down, where everything took place at night, and I was very moved by the situation of these children, who were fine if they lived in the dark but could not join the day-lit world.


JOANNA SCOTT

So far in my years as a writer, I have had a lot of ideas, and a lot of dead ends. So I find myself writing in one direction and then another, and sometimes it clicks and sometimes it doesn't. I feel there has to be a certain amount of improvisation as I'm writing, which means any idea or any commitment to a project is risky. It involves time, it involves gathering of material, and sometimes it just doesn't work. Sometimes it does. As I'm starting out on a project, I can't tell if it will click or not, if it will keep generating its own future, in a sense.

It partly has to do with the independence of the characters, the strength of their voices. If I feel there's a distinct voice that deserves to keep speaking, that has a music of its own, a rhythm of its own, then I find myself seduced by the voice that I've created. It's almost as though I'm hearing it from elsewhere.

There's a point I set for myself—and it's an arbitrary point—when I think no matter what happens I'm going to finish that book. And that's when I get to page 100. I have to see it out.

## TIM PARKS

Usually what happens is there'll be some kernel of plot in the head, a basic story, for a couple of years, and what's happening is, it's waiting for another story that will mix with it, and in particular, the right setting that will give it sense. So, with *Europa*, I had the plot of the atrocious betrayal and obsession in my head for over a year before I realized it had to mesh with the bus trip to the European Parliament.

## COLM TÓIBÍN

For *The Master*, about Henry James, I was looking for a moment of public drama, and the opening of his play *Guy Domville* was the main one in Henry James's life. It's much easier to write about failure than about success. And how he dealt with that night shows a great deal about his character. He put the same hopes into a play as a contemporary writer might into a film script or a film project. He thought he could clean up. The play was an unmitigated disaster, its opening night a great public humiliation.

## CAROLYN PARKHURST

I start with the characters first. For *The Dogs of Babel*, I had an image in my mind of a man whose wife has died, and I knew that, as he tries to figure out exactly what happened, he'd be looking back on their marriage, which was often wonderful but also quite troubled. That was the first part of the book that I had. But it also seemed to me that, in his grief, my character might do something a little off-balance in his search for answers. Around that time, I happened to come across a strange little piece I'd written in graduate school about talking dogs, and I thought, "Well, that's a little off-balance." It kind of just all came together.

## MARISHA PESSL

The structure of *Special Topics in Calamity Physics* really evolved around the main character, Blue. I always start my stories and novels with character, and in this particular case her voice began to emerge for me, this incredibly shy, bookish person. And due to the nomadic nature of her childhood—for ten years she and her father, Gareth, have traveled around America—she has no friendships beyond that of her father and the books that she reads. And it's through these books that she interprets the world.

So the structure of the novel comes organically from her voice, the constant references and the way she decides to structure her life story through the chapter titles. And because she's so scientific and she loves clear and unambiguous labeling, then it would make sense to structure the novel itself through these books, which are really a part of her childhood.

The structure was never intimidating or off-putting, simply because this was Blue's character, and the references are meant to be humorous as much as painful. To read about a character who at least initially sees the world purely through books is heartbreaking and funny. The references purposefully thin out through the novel as Blue learns to live life rather than read about it.

## RUSSELL BANKS

I work very differently from John Irving, on the one hand, inasmuch as I try not to know my last sentences. But I also work very differently from, say, Michael Ondaatje, author of *The English Patient*, who does write in the scattershot, or shotgun, way, without knowing really where one sentence will lead to the next, or how. I fall somewhere in between these two. And I generally work with a very loose, big, and infinitely changeable outline for the overall narrative arc of the novel and at the same time a more detailed and refined outline that covers the next chapter or perhaps twenty or thirty pages.

## JOYCE CAROL OATES

I always rewrite the very beginning of a novel. I rewrite the beginning as I write the ending, so I may spend part of the morning writing the ending—the last hundred pages approximately—and then part of the morning revising the beginning. So the style of the novel has a consistency. And often, I'm changing the beginning because of what the ending has led me to. The beginnings are always changed many, many times. I probably rewrite the first chapter twenty times, because my vision of the novel is evolving.

# 2

# Haven't I Seen You Somewhere Before?

## *How Characters Come to Life*

Occasionally, characters in a novel seem so vivid that it's hard to believe they're not real people. The voice of Holden Caulfield rings so clear and true that it's easy to become convinced that there must have been a teenager living on J. D. Salinger's street who inspired the book, or that he based the character on himself. He can't be merely a figment of the imagination.

And so readers query Alice McDermott about whether the "Charming Billy" in her novel of the same name was based on a relative, and they ask Richard Ford who Frank Bascombe really is.

Writers admit that they sometimes base their characters on real people. But if so, they usually adopt one person's laugh, another's penchant for burning toast, a third one's habit of tapping his fingers when he's nervous. In the process, they create another person altogether.

Even historical figures are not the nonfiction portraits of a biographer, but a different animal altogether—a character writers create for their own purposes, who may not be like the real person at all.

And sometimes, characters come out of thin air—a voice in the writer's head that demands to be written down. Walter Mosley says Easy Rawlins appeared in that way. He didn't even know the character's name when he started writing.

## WALTER MOSLEY

I didn't grow up with Easy Rawlins, and I am certainly not Easy Rawlins. I once started a story from the first-person point of view but I didn't know who the first person was. It started like this: "His name was Raymond, but we called him Mouse, because he was small and sharp-featured. We could have called him Rat, because he really wasn't very nice. But we liked him, and so the name Mouse stuck." Later in the story, Mouse enters and sees my unknown narrator, and says, "Hey, Easy, how you doin'?" That's where Easy Rawlins comes from.

## CHARLES BAXTER

Before starting *The Feast of Love*, I had been to a middle-school production of *A Midsummer Night's Dream*, and it occurred to me that it might be possible to write a book in something of a hybrid form: a novel of voices, a novel that was halfway to being a play. I started by writing the voices of Diana and a character named Jonah, who dropped out of the story. It began as a rather dark and grim narrative, and I wasn't happy about the way it was going until Chloe entered it. She provided the humor—and the bawdy quality of romantic/

sexual life—that I thought the story really needed. Her humor seemed to attach itself to Bradley, who became a bit more funny himself. Chloe came to life, for me, almost from the moment she appeared on the page, when Oscar tells her she's "underpierced." She's quite certain of herself, and she had (for me) a sharp, smart, and sometimes loud voice. I miss her.

## MARISHA PESSL

My characters are not thinly veiled portraits of people in my personal life. I love to invent characters out of nothing and make them real, so people believe them to actually exist.

Strangers that I encounter, that I observe in a waiting room or riding a bus, or have some sort of fleeting encounter with—whether it's a professor I had, in the case of Gareth, or a very shy person that I once observed in terms of Blue— these kinds of strangers inspire me to create characters rather than people in my own life. Not knowing them allows me to invent their histories, their joys and sorrows.

At the same time, writing is a sort of acting exercise. You have to bring yourself and your own sensibility to your character, and yet you must diminish or augment certain aspects of yourself, see the world through their eyes, and judge the world according to their moral compass.

I took an acting class at a studio in New York called Stella Adler Studio, and one of my teachers was Stella herself, who of course taught Marlon Brando. And this teacher said that Brando would go to Central Park and would watch people for hours, and this is how he would create his characters, including Vito Corleone. And I started doing that after taking this class. It's in tiny details—someone's bitten fingernails or the way they stoop as they walk—it's in those details that human quality is revealed. And I used that with my own characterizations.

## RICHARD FORD

Frank Bascombe's not anybody. He's a piece of language, really, which has a sound that the reader can hear when he or she silently reads that language aloud. He isn't a person at all. As a piece of artifice, he's an instrument whereby I can as a writer get as much as I know, and can make up, and imagine, and that seems as pertinent to what I think my book is about, as possible. I think that for me, Frank Bascombe stays—as I'm writing him, and up to the last—entirely mutable and perhaps even impressionistic, whereas for a reader, I think he seems not mutable and quite specific. At least that's my understanding of what characters do. They exist differently in the minds of the people who write them from how they exist in the minds of the people who read them. I should say that this is not in any way to denigrate "his" aesthetic usefulness.

No, I don't remember when he first walked on the page. Absolutely I know where he came from. He came from a kind of collusion between my own imagination and several books that I cared and do care very deeply about. In that way he's a sort of received voice, which got altered by my use amid various origins.

## MARY KAY ZURAVLEFF

As for the characters in *The Bowl Is Already Broken*, the former director of the Freer/Sackler Gallery in Washington,

DC, gave me one of the highest compliments to date, when he wrote me that, "It's amazing we didn't know these people at the museum—because we might have."

Some people have said they think they recognize someone but someone else's words are coming out of his/her mouth. I don't think they're right, because I needed characters to tell my story, and that wasn't a story that had played out with the people I knew.

## ELIZABETH GRAVER

In all my writing, I'm trying to portray characters who are complicated, flawed, trying to find their way. I am not interested in easy divides between good and evil, any more than I am interested in easy happy endings, tying things up with a bow. I *am* interested in inner life, and in strong emotions; my characters tend to feel a lot—they are not the reticent, held-back, wordless characters of minimalism. In this way, I perhaps tip toward the danger of being sentimental, in that I am inside "sentiment" a lot, or perhaps we might be allowed to call it "emotion." That's what interests me—what people think and feel, and how those thoughts and feelings are at once private and, at times, able to be communicated. I don't want to shy away from emotion, any more than I want to close things down by offering too much resolution or painting a rosy picture.

I just taught *Mrs. Dalloway* to my students. At one point, Woolf writes that Clarissa Dalloway could "never say of someone that they were this or they were that." It's that kind of complexity I am after.

## JHUMPA LAHIRI

It's a fact about my writing that I write about characters of a certain background. But I don't see them as Indian-American characters. I don't see through that screen of difference. Sometimes people ask me, "Did you grow up eating Indian food?" And I don't think of it as Indian food. I think of it as food. So it's the same with my characters. I just think of them as characters, as people. I think it's inevitable that readers will ask me these questions, given that I live in a country where Indians are not a majority.

I'm never speaking for all Indian Americans, or all Bengali Americans for that matter. These are just individual characters brought up in a particular way, as everyone is. I would caution a reader not to draw general conclusions about how people live based on a character in my book. I will say that Gogol and Sonia, in my novel *The Namesake*, are sort of based on a collective body of people I knew when I was growing up, and an invention of many different people I knew.

## ALICE McDERMOTT

The great benefit of writing about Irish Catholics is that they're all alike (the Irish are indeed an island race). I once gave a reading from *At Weddings and Wakes*, and at the Q & A someone asked, "Is this your family you're writing about?" Before I could answer, someone from the other side of the room shouted, "No, it's mine!" But then again, I had a letter from a reader of *Charming Billy* who said that if I changed all the surnames in the novel, and changed the alcohol to high-cholesterol food, I'd be writing about his Jewish family.

## E. L. DOCTOROW

I find that the people in my fiction come to me whole, their physical nature, their diction, their histories, all of a piece, and each of them unique and special in my mind. . . . In *Sweet Land Stories*, while in one of the stories people are particularly murderous, they are that with a sense of their resolute normality—that this is the way they live so as to perfect their lives. The other people in the stories seem to be trying to improve their station in life, or find some meaning in themselves, and I think I deal with them and their imperfections with some compassion. If there's any insight to be gained from the scoundrels in the first story, it is that evil is always committed with the sense of righteous self-justification.

## RUSSELL BANKS

Neither Wade Whitehouse in *Affliction* nor Bob Dubois in *Continental Drift* is based on any particular person. However, I have known men like both characters all my life, and in fact am related to a number of men like them. And so naturally, I drew on that knowledge and those relationships in writing those novels. All fictional characters are in a sense composites made up of people known intimately and only casually and sometimes only through other fictional characters, transformed through the process of writing into unique—one hopes, unique—characters. It's dangerous and misleading to view characters in fiction as portraits of people in the author's life.

In both *Cloudsplitter* and *The Darling*, it seemed to me natural and therefore necessary to include historical figures, because the characters I was writing about were themselves involved with historical figures, and if not personally involved, they were very aware of their existence. To me, historical figures are no more and no less a part of the context in a story than the physical circumstance or place. To me, for example, if Liberia is a real country, and it is a setting for a novel, and there's no problem with that, then why not include Charles Taylor and President Samuel Doe, and even John Kerry, who makes a cameo appearance.

For E. L. Doctorow, they're more like images that he builds into a collage and fictional environment, whereas for me they are genuine characters. John Brown exists in our imagination almost on a mythical level, which is why I needed the intervening narrator of his son Owen, because John Brown is almost too large, and iconic, a figure for us to see—unless we have someone who knows him as a human being tell us about him.

In *The Darling,* Hannah is, in one sense, that darling: privileged, spoiled, and entitled. But the word *darling* means many things in English. It's an allusion also to Chekhov's story "The Darling," which is an affectionate portrait of a narcissist, a very difficult thing to do. But it is one of the things I was trying to do with this novel. I feel personally affectionate toward Hannah, although I'm very aware of her limitations. I think sometimes we want to either idealize our characters in fiction or judge them—especially, perhaps, when it comes to female characters. But the only truly believable characters are flawed, but not so terribly flawed that we reject them. I wonder how we would feel toward Hannah if Hannah were a man. Because there's nothing that Hannah does, except bear children, that a man could not do. I suspect if Hannah were a man, the reader would see him as a Hemingwayesque, stoical existential hero searching for meaning in a meaningless world and morality in an amoral world.

COLM TÓIBÍN

I began by having no interest in the life of Henry James. The four novels of his that I read from the age of about nineteen— and I did not study them at university, I read them for pleasure, they meant a great deal to me—are *The Portrait of a Lady*, *The Wings of the Dove*, *The Ambassadors*, and *The Golden Bowl*. And I certainly went through my twenties and thirties rereading them, thinking about them, and talking to people about them.

I was intrigued, then, when I started to read about his life, at just its contours and its textures. I didn't know what I was going to do about it, and then I realized I had a character in my head, just the way I do before a novel. And I set to work.

Between about 1909 and 1912, James suffered a number of nervous breakdowns. I see his later years, including the years of my novel, as a buildup to the nervous breakdowns. I realize that the *New York Times* reviewer wondered if James in fact, because of his public persona, was a brighter person, more content and easygoing, and I emphatically doubt that, if you can emphatically doubt something. I think, like a lot of people who are witty in public, this is often a way of disguising a darkness within. I believe there was a great deal of darkness. And I sought to explore that darkness.

Had it not been there, I might have invented it. But I didn't invent it. I would have, I think, but I didn't.


MARIE ARANA

Don Victor is partly my father. Certainly, my father was an engineer. And a brilliant one.

But Don Victor is also my husband, a wonderfully stubborn, hardheaded, softhearted man.

And Don Victor is my great uncle Tio Salvador, a bemedaled admiral in the Peruvian navy, who was half insane and trooped off to Andorra to try to become king.

And Don Victor is me, too. Loving his family beyond expression. And yet dragging them where they should not go.

Of course, he became his own person.

And a stubborn one, too.

I remember my editor saying that she didn't think that Don Victor would be capable of doing this or that thing I had him do, and when I thought about editing these things, he got huffy and arrogant about it.

So really: Characters will do what they have to do. We pull them from experience, but then they go off and do whatever in creation they want to.

Like one's children.


ALISON SMITH

It took me six years to write *Name All the Animals*, and I consider it my PhD program. I didn't get an advanced degree, I just rewrote *Name All the Animals* eighteen times until it was readable. It took me a long time to really get at the heart of the matter, because it was painful to look at that material— my brother's death when I was a teenager. The first draft was eight hundred pages long . . . and I didn't appear in it. I didn't see myself as a part of my family story. I discovered it's really, really hard to write a memoir if you're not a character in it. In order to make my writing work, I had to face the reality that I had allowed myself to be erased from the story. Sibling grief is an incredibly overlooked loss. The accepted standard of the most horrible thing that can happen to you is the death of your child. I can't really argue with that. But I don't know a single person who has lost a brother or sister who hasn't heard this phrase: "It's your job now to look after your parents." When I started writing the book, I had reached a point where people would say, "Do you have any brothers or sisters?" And I would say, "My parents lost a child." I didn't see my own loss. But the truth was I was living in a sea of loss, drowning in it. And no one was acknowledging this.

And so it was an extraordinarily important experience for me to become the main character, and to understand if you write a memoir, the only thing you have going for you is your point of view. It doesn't matter how ordinary or scandalous your life was. What matters is your point of view on what happened to you.

## DOREEN BAINGANA

For the stories from a young girl's perspective, I was trying my level best to get into a child's voice without making it childish. Since the stories are somewhat autobiographical, I was looking back to how I felt, how I thought, how I reacted to things as a child, and trying to capture the insightfulness of children and innocence—and I didn't want to condescend. And otherwise, I think I just tried my best, as we all do.

## PAM HOUSTON

I am a dog lover. I had an Irish wolfhound named Dante who appeared in my life at the exact right moment and taught me many of the things I needed to know about the relationship between love and loss, and how to keep getting up in the morning. He was diagnosed with bone cancer on his fourth birthday, and going through his treatment, remission, and eventual recurrence and death was one of the most powerful experiences of my life.

What I wanted in *Sight Hound* was a community of voices telling the story. I had seen the play *The Laramie Project*, about Matthew Shepard's death, and the actors stepped forward and delivered monologues about that night. In *Sight Hound*, many characters tell the story—a veterinarian, a hockey player, an actor, a vet student. It seemed only right that Dante would speak on his own behalf.


MARGOT LIVESEY

A son of a friend was diagnosed in the early 1990s with Asperger's syndrome, about which at that time I knew virtually nothing, although Asperger's was first diagnosed about fifty years ago. Watching my friend's son and watching him grow up, I became very fascinated by this condition, and I wanted for a number of years to write something about a character who has this. So I started, as it were, auditioning the character for a role in my novels. I decided he couldn't be the person to find a baby in the bus station in *Criminals*, and he couldn't be the person to keep his girlfriend prisoner in *The Missing World*. Finally, after nearly a decade, I decided he needed his own novel. And I thought that novel, *Banishing Verona*, ought to take place in the territory where people with Asperger's had the most difficulty—that is, dealing with relationships and social interactions.

## MARTIN AMIS

John Updike once asked: What is it about fictional characters that we respond to? After all, we love brutes and rogues and vamps. His answer was that what we like is *life*. If they're alive, then we will like them, no matter what they do. I adore all my characters indiscriminately, like my children, but I have no favorites.

# What's It All About?

## *The Ideas Behind the Stories*

Start talking about theme and it feels like you're in an English literature class, discussing how fear and shame were an undercurrent in . . . , and how latent homosexuality was central to . . .

It's rare to come across a fiction writer who starts off with a "big idea" in mind. Want to write about the effect of birth control on feminism? Try writing nonfiction.

Sometimes writers make a conscious decision to write about a situation that allows them to explore themes—first-time novelist Claire Tristram did this in her book *After*, about 9/11. At other times, they happen upon ideas haphazardly—although of course Freud would say there is no such thing as an accident.

Virtually all writers bring out themes once they've discovered them in the process of writing, working back and forth between the conscious and the subconscious as they become increasingly aware of what their story "is about." Those themes can become so compelling that they run through all

of an author's work. I remember my writing adviser in graduate school pointing out that I was working on a lot of stories about fathers; I cringed, waiting for him to tell me I was
repeating myself, but he said: "Keep mining that."

And so Russell Banks writes about race, and Margot
Livesey about "bad behavior," and Gish Jen about identity.
Their obsessions are their themes, and they turn them over
and over, examining them from one side and another until,
by the time they're finished, "lit crit" majors do have an awful
lot to dissect. But their analyses won't resemble the much
more intuitive artistic process that brought those themes to
light.

## MARGOT LIVESEY

I think, like many writers, I'm quite fascinated by bad behavior, both the bad behavior that comes with inattention—
which I wrote about in *Criminals*—and the much more
active and self-interested bad behavior of a character like
Henry in *Banishing Verona*. And I think the other side of that
fascination is that I'm very interested in how people will tol-
erate extremely bad behavior if they feel that they're the one
exception to the bad behavior. How sometimes we feel particularly flattered when someone who is obnoxious to someone else is nice to us. And I think I'm also very fascinated
with how much one can get away with if one is sufficiently
charming and sufficiently bold.

Part of what interested me about Henry is that he doesn't
think of himself as behaving particularly badly. To him, the
great pursuit of a sort of "Henry-dom" justifies plagiarism,
embezzling, financial misdealings. It all makes perfect sense to

him. And I think such people put the rest of us who operate by different rules at a remarkable disadvantage.

I think Jonathan in *The Missing World* is clearly one of Henry's immediate ancestors, and it's hard to live in the contemporary world without being forced to ponder how it is that people can behave badly in so many different spheres— from the blatantly personal to the much more impersonal such as Enron or some of our leaders.

## ART SPIEGELMAN

*Maus* dealt with events forty or more years past. *In the Shadow of No Towers* was made in the midst of rubble. My parents were victims. I'm glad to say my family was only a close-up witness to these events, which were ultimately far smaller in scale. The main similarity is just that I found myself at the intersection where personal history and world history cross. My goal in *Maus* was to stay out of the way of the narrative so that the visual elements are invisible to anyone who chooses not to look carefully. These *No Towers* pages require a high degree of visual attention, or a much "harder" read, and they don't offer the "easy" pleasures—if that's the right word—of an uninterrupted narrative ride.

## RUSSELL BANKS

I felt fairly early in my life, in my late teens and early twenties, that the story of race was central to the American imagination and had been since the sixteenth century, when the first Europeans arrived in this hemisphere. And inasmuch as I am an American, and participate in that imagination, then race is central to my understanding of myself. Therefore, I feel obliged to make race central to my work.

With *The Darling*, I wasn't so much interested in writing about Africa as I was in writing about Liberia, the reason being that Liberia is an important chapter in the American story of race, and that's the story I want to write about. I was also interested in Liberia because it is our unacknowledged colony in Africa and has been since its creation in about 1820. And I wanted to expose the hypocrisy of our denial of having any colony in Africa and our avoidance of any responsibility for the social and political chaos in that region.

One thing I'm very interested in, in an ongoing way, is the unintended consequence of good intentions. And you can see that most particularly perhaps in *The Darling*, but also in *Cloudsplitter*, and going back even farther to *Continental Drift* or *Affliction*. *The Sweet Hereafter* I think deals with other themes, perhaps mainly with how one copes with the inexplicable loss of a child or a loved one. Whom do you blame? The question of blame is central to that novel but not necessarily to the others.

I can see, however, that it's related to the theme of unintended consequences, because when things turn out tragically different from the way one intended, whom do you blame? As in Iraq, for instance.


CLAIRE TRISTRAM

In my novel *After*, I'm dealing very directly with a theme, and the theme is the psychological fallout of living in a post–9/11 world. And I chose the story very directly to illustrate my theme. I guess my story is something so completely on my mind—what it means to be an American right now, what's happening in the world, and what's going to happen next—and that's probably one of the reasons I wrote it very quickly. I chose to characterize it in such an individual way. I have two main characters and focus on their experiences. The passion for the story came from wanting to write about the world today.

## JOHN DALTON

I don't write with a theme in mind. Everything comes out of character, and usually, when I've got the right characters and the right event, it will suggest a scene. I very much like writing scenes. But it often takes a great deal of time for me to understand exactly what thematic ideas the scene is suggesting.

## JOYCE CAROL OATES

It can be said that many human endeavors depend upon a "quarrel" with reality, whether these are scientific or philosophical or political or aesthetic. I think that, like many writers, I'm fascinated by the world that surrounds me, both the human world and the world of nature. I don't know that I have a quarrel with it, but I do see myself as an observer, both admiring and skeptical.

## ALICE McDERMOTT

I suppose I've never set out to write a novel in which nothing happens . . . only to write a novel about the lives of certain characters. That nothing "happens" in their lives is beside the point to me; I'm still interested in how they live, and think, and speak, and make some sense of their own experience. Incident (in novels and in life) is momentary, and temporary, but the memory of an incident, the story told about it, the meaning it takes on or loses over time, is lifelong and fluid, and that's what interests me and what I hope will prove interesting to readers. We're deluged with stories of things that have happened, events, circumstances, actions, etc. We need some stories that reveal how we think and feel and hope and dream.

## DOREEN BAINGANA

I began most of the stories with certain incidents that I wanted to explore. As I did, I realized that I was actually asking myself certain questions that I hoped to answer in the story. As the story progressed, in answering these questions, I was addressing the themes of culture, of race, but also themes that arise out of family love, how that can be difficult and exhilarating at the same time.

I think fiction, perhaps as a side effect, can be educational, but I don't write to teach people. I just write to answer questions for myself and hope to reveal some truth. If people learn something from it, that's great.

## MARIE ARANA

I wanted to write a book about people who believe in magic—who have deep spiritual ties to their faith and beliefs—but who aren't being given one whit of magic in their lives. If you look closely at *Cellophane*, you'll see that it's all based on science. There isn't one levitating moment.

I greatly admire García Márquez, Cervantes, Cortázar,

Borges. You'll see a bit of that admiration, I guess, in my work.

For the daughter of an engineer, as I was, science is magical.

Magic for me is something that lives in human heads. We long for it. We wait for it. And sometimes it happens. But, of course, it is all up there, somewhere between the cortex and the hippocampus. But that doesn't make the magic less real.

Cortázar wrote a beautiful essay, "El real magico," or something like that (can't remember the exact word, but it wasn't *magico*, come to think of it), in which he explained that for those of us who grew up in South America, where extremes are so common, it is only natural for us to see magic in the hard world around us.

Also, for all the truth we tell, and for however hard it is to tell it, no one can ever know what is in our hearts—what that truth we want to tell really is. No one can live in our skin. And we all see things from our corner of the cave.

This is an observation I've made, and it figures large in *Cellophane*.

MARY KAY ZURAVLEFF

I started *The Bowl Is Already Broken* in 1995 with both an image and a question. The image was that of a bowl tumbling down the stairs of a museum and breaking into a million pieces. The question, or questions, were: How do things become valuable? What sacrifices are we willing to make to preserve the things we've deemed valuable? And what if you make extraordinary sacrifices, and whatever you've put up on a pedestal falls and is destroyed?

I consider this book a love letter to museums, warts and all.

Because it's not a diatribe or an exposé, I didn't think folks would be too upset. Still. Most have been lovely and excited, and they applaud my airing some of the complicated ethical questions they have to wrestle with in real life. Many have enjoyed the humor, and a few have been a little protective of their turf.

## DAN CHAON

I think my purpose in writing the novel *You Remind Me of Me* was to look at the questions of nurture and nature—not necessarily to find an answer to the question of what turns us into the people that we are but to try to get deeper into the mystery of that. I don't think it's one or the other. As an adoptee myself, I've seen both sides of the coin. Parts of me are definitely genetic; parts of me are definitely a result of my upbringing; and other parts appear to be my own invention.

## JHUMPA LAHIRI

My intention with *The Namesake* was to write a story about a family adapting to a life in a new world. As a result, I'm talking about the existence of different cultures and how they intersect and sometimes don't intersect. But I don't have a specific commentary on cultures per se. I think that's something a reader might bring to the work. But I think my work does highlight the value and significance of tradition and culture to individuals, and that is a universal feeling—we all yearn to feel at home in the world.

The entire novel was inspired by the fact that I knew someone named Gogol. It got me thinking about the names we have, and why we have them, and the people who give them to us, and how names can mean very different things in different parts of the world. I meditated on these things for several years, and I tried to bring some of those thoughts to the novel, which is very much about searching for identity. And names obviously speak so much about who we are.

GISH JEN

I do write about identity, because I am a bicultural person, and the writer in me understands that to be a tremendous gift. I understand I have been blessed with a lens through which I can look at the world, American identity, what a nation is. Interesting questions. I think I am no different from the inventor of the telescope. Once you realize you have a telescope, you just want to know everything you can do with it. I'm aware that this lens is not as exciting for some people as it is for me. Certainly, if they are more excited about horse racing, they should write about that. But I am fascinated by cultural difference, and the role that ethnicity has in shaping our twenty-first century reality. I feel very lucky to be able to be part of the conversation around these matters.

I have never felt more proud than when I was asked after the publication of *Mona in the Promised Land* what I was doing for the High Holy Days. It is also true that when I answered, as I had to, "Nothing," I felt guilty and lapsed. Not sure whether it was Jewish guilt or Chinese guilt, but it was guilt.

FRANCES ITANI

Language has always been important to me throughout childhood and adulthood, and now, as a writer, it's really the most important thing. For sure, I wanted language to be one of the important focuses of *Deafening*. In the novel, Grania's grandmother, Mamo, in fact, saves Grania's life twice, and the first way she does so is through the gift of language.

Thematically, I was working with several issues. Sound and silence were important from the beginning, and I tried to balance the various parts of the book so that in the background, the reader is always aware of these two concepts. Sound, of course, as I learned in my research, is not important at all to deaf people. Sound, as my character says, is more important to the hearing. In my book, the sound of artillery is devastating to the young soldiers who take part in World War I. I learned while reading hundreds of journals, diaries, documents, and letters that every man who was at that war wrote home about sound.

MAUREEN HOWARD

There's a great deal of silence in *The Silver Screen*. Hidden stories, stories never told, secrets of life. And one of the things that I was interested in, in terms of the silent screen, was the fact that Bel, who has a career set up in silents and has made a name for herself, comes to the point where she has to cross over into talkies, and I was interested to make sure that it was understood that she could easily have crossed over. So many actors and actresses could not, but she could have, and chose not to. Her choosing not to is turning away from a life and a career. To put it very simply, as she does to the young woman who attaches herself to Bel, the photographer Gemma, she says very clearly, "It was not my life." And the choice is again spelled out, I think very clearly, though people have wondered about it, like Gemma. Why did you give it up when you were about to be a star? When the big thing was there for you? Because it was a moral decision. It was a choice, a moral choice, not to go with that life she had been leading, not to go with the Hollywood life.

And the book has some miracles in it. The one miracle here is that when she does the test for her voice for the studio, for MGM, she hears her mother's voice as she sees herself on screen speaking. She hears her dead mother's voice, and the text of the mother's admonition is, "You will never be horrid, will you?" And of course she feels that she has been living a false and somewhat horrid life. And so it's really all there, and therefore the idea of silent movies and talkies—the idea of silencing oneself, in this case.

I think that the performance, the idea of ourselves as performers, is important, and there is a way in which writers are performing. They may not think of it that way, but there is a kind of performing self, which can block reality. It can block the real role that you should be fulfilling in life, or might want to fulfill in life. Seeing yourself as a part of mass culture might be to many horrifying. But of course, one of the things in the book, which isn't really written about celebrity—I was thinking more of our public and private lives, and in a sense how we live through the years the small history of our personal lives against the backdrop of history, which dwarfs or sets our own performance in perspective.

ELIZABETH GRAVER

I think *Awake* is partly about learning to alter your vision and trying to see in a new way—to see lightness in dark, to risk sounding clichéd; to be able to imagine a world that, while it looks claustrophobic from the outside, contains its own gifts. Life brings you challenges you don't expect, and then, if you can, you try to live gracefully and with courage inside them. Anna is neither particularly graceful nor particularly coura- geous in the novel. I think she is thorny, complicated, flawed. But that interested me; I wanted to write about someone who did *not* grow easily accustomed to the dark but who was nevertheless asking important questions, flailing about, mak- ing mistakes and then trying to make sense of what she had done. I don't think she arrives at a clarity of vision by the end of the book, but she is struggling toward that, figuring out if and how she can accept the "darkness" in both a metaphori- cal and a literal way. For her, that means accepting that her son could die; it means accepting the limitations and gifts of her family life and looking hard at the repercussions of her own actions. It also, though, means, I think, finding ways to "see" anew in the dark, to find her way back to her art, to rediscover pieces of herself she had set aside and find a kind of "night vision."

## A. S. BYATT

Most writers are better at treating big moral issues obliquely, unless they are completely possessed by something they must say. I am suspicious of writers who go looking for issues to address. Writers are neither preachers nor journalists. Journalists know much more than most writers about what's going on in the world. And if you want to change things, you do journalism.

Books I have read that were written at a moment of social- political crisis tend to be incomprehensible twenty years later. Books that are written about some problem of twenty or fifty or a hundred years ago are written with understanding and somehow also illuminate the present and the future.

# Truth or Dare?

## *Changing Facts to Make a*
## *Story More Real*

Novelists and short-story writers often face the frustrating question: "But is it true?" As if that is what makes a story authentic. As if the fact that it really happened would make the story better.

Yet there is a fascinating connection between truth and imagination that writers exploit all the time as they strive to make their stories, whether fiction or nonfiction, believable. The line drawn is especially wiggly in fiction—if a line is drawn at all.

Some writers, such as Richard Bausch, make up absolutely everything—the black beret a former husband wears, a woman turning on the water in a hotel room to drown out her sister's crying. Others admit to using the truth—but changing it around. Charles Baxter quite purposefully gives his own insomnia to one of the narrators of *The Feast of Love*—and then names him Charlie Baxter. But is that Charles Baxter the writer? Yes, and no. Edward P. Jones said that one fact—that blacks had owned slaves—gave him the "license" to create the fiction that gives life to *The Known World*.

But always, the truth, in fiction, must be greater than the sum of its facts. Joanna Scott quotes Daniel Defoe: "What I'm writing here is truer than history." It's a goal to which all of the writers in this book aspire.


## RICHARD BAUSCH

It's all imagination. It's all made up. I never use any models. There's an explanation of that, that's a little complicated to say, but it has to do with Flannery O'Connor's comment that a good story is literal in the same sense that a child's drawing is literal. And if I'm making it up completely, it's a child's drawing. If you're making up a room for a story, whatever your subconscious presents you with to say about this room probably has to do with the concerns of the story precisely because it occurs to you to say it. If you're writing about a room you've been in, you have the problem of selection. There was a spittoon there, should I mention that? So that's how I mean it. It's just made up. You just make it up, and trust it.

But then, having dreamed it up, you have to go through it, and through it, and through it, and through it over and over again, getting to know about it a little bit more each time. Getting smarter every time. Until it's done. And even then, you don't know everything that's there. You just trust that it is.


## DOREEN BAINGANA

I like to quote a writer who asked, Is this story a fact? No. But is it true? Yes. I'm trying to get to the emotional truth.

So, some of what I write about is based on experiences I have had. But to get to the emotional truth, I have had to move away from what actually happened to what I wanted to have happened in the story. As a small example, I have six sisters in real life, and they told me not to write about them. But when there were only three sisters in *Tropical Fish*, my sisters complained. So you can't win.

## JOANNA SCOTT

I often write about the past, partly because it's different. It requires discovery. So I go to the past to learn something. I think I like to imagine a fictional reality for an actual reality that's been lost. Just as I try to give voices to characters who can no longer speak, I try to animate something that once existed. In a sense, I'm trying to animate the dead. I can't do that, so I move into the fables, the make-believe, of fiction, where we all know, readers and writers, that the ghosts are inventions. But it's a wonderful pretense.

Telling ourselves that fiction is true and at the same time not true is essential to the art of fiction. It's been at the heart of fiction from the start. Fiction can persuade us with its truths, yet we know it's based on a flat-out lie. Sometimes it drives novelists mad. Sometimes it energizes us. I like to think of it as a mathematical problem we have to deal with, something we keep trying to solve.

I love seeing in early novels a declaration of truth. Defoe claims, "What I'm writing here is truer than history." It takes a lot of bravado to say that, and it also poses a puzzle. We need to think about the action of interpretation when a writer who is lying tells us he is telling the truth. But it's an exciting stance, for both readers and writers. And it becomes more complex as we grow older and become more mature readers. I feel as a writer, I'm addressing this in each book a little bit more precisely or deeply or obsessively.


## EDWARD P. JONES

I think *The Known World* is probably ninety-eight percent fiction. When I was in college, I first heard that there were black slaveholders, so that was a fact. With that fact, I had a license to create a fictional world. I threw in a few names here and there—people such as Benjamin Franklin and George Washington—but those are very minor and it's only in passing that I mention them.

I started out thinking I would read a whole bunch of books about slavery. But I never got around to doing that. I kept putting it all off. I started thinking about reading the books in 1992, but while I was putting off the research, I was also crafting the novel in my head. So in 2001, after almost ten years of thinking about the novel, I had about five weeks of vacation with the day job I had then, and I decided that I could either spend that vacation time and the next year or so reading all those books or I could just go with the novel that was in my head. Everything was in my head except for about twelve pages.

In life, you accumulate facts about the world and about history as you go through your life. And I figured I knew enough about 1855 Virginia to write the novel. And as I said last night at a bookstore, if I say it's 1855 Virginia, then you'll believe me until I say something to contradict that.

## FRANCES ITANI

As a fiction writer, my job is to create story, but because *Deafening* is set during a particular period, I had to do factual research so that I could learn the social and cultural history of the times. In the book, I tried to stay true to actual happenings at the school for the deaf, and for sure, the war scenes are set in real time for the period.

What is made up is the entire story, and all of the characters. But the reason I did so much research was to make sure that each small detail, which helps to ground the story, is entirely accurate.

The really difficult part for the writer is to try to remain as subtle as possible during the storytelling. Focus has to be on story and story line, and not on the information one has researched. So even though an enormous amount of research must be done to authenticate historical setting, etc., this really helps the writer to feel comfortable in the period and comfortable with the language of the times, but the trick—if there is a trick—is to make the information almost disappear and allow detail to emerge through story and character.

## WALTER MOSLEY

I was recently on a panel of advisers for new screenplay writers at the Sundance Institute in Utah. I was the only novelist among the group of ten writers. What astonished me was that the screenplay writers do a lot more research than most novelists I know, which is very interesting. Because in one aspect, screenplay writers have taken up the mantle of nineteenth- and early-twentieth-century writers—that is, to bring the foreign and technical world to the layman. Most current novels are about characters and the psyche, and with those historical exceptions, require less specific research. The rule of thumb in writing fiction is that while you're writing, if you come across some subject that you find yourself ignorant of, you'd better find out what that something is.


RICHARD FORD

I try to do as little research as possible, but sometimes I just have a plan for a book that bumps me up against things I don't know. And then I have to resort to my very suspect reportorial skills. By the time I'm writing a book, I'm so keen to be writing it that I hate to stop and take two weeks and go learn something that I didn't know but that I have to know. But I do it. For me, subjects really have to engage my imagination, not just be backed up by reporting.


ANTHONY DOERR

For this novel, *About Grace*, I did tons of book research—everything from dreams to snow to the Yukon, the history of the Grenadine islands, also travel. I had spent time in the Caribbean and in Alaska, but I also went back once the book was in progress. All that research—maybe a third research, a third experience, and a third imagination.

I don't have a formal background in science—I get asked that question all the time. I studied history and English in college, got a master's in writing, but I was always sort of an autodidact in science. My mom is a high-school science teacher, and one of my brothers works in optics at Bell Labs, so I was always surrounded by it. For example, when we were kids we would go to the beach. My parents would drive us to Florida every spring—in a big, old, rusty Suburban—and we'd collect stuff on the beach for our big saltwater aquarium back in Ohio. Every time we found anything, any mollusk, my mom would bring out the guidebook and quiz us on what it was, so that stuff was built in early. I never played inside as a kid—even in the rain, I'd go out. So I think that's where my attention still goes. I think that's why I love to write about that stuff.

## PAUL AUSTER

The story that is told by Trause to Sidney toward the end of the novel *Oracle Night* is a true story. I didn't put in the name of the writer, but the facts as I know them are very, very close to what's in the novel. A man wrote a narrative poem about a drowning child, and not long after the book was published, his own child drowns. Now of course, as Sidney responds initially, it's just a terrible, terrible coincidence. At the same time, in a state of grief and wretchedness, it's perfectly understandable that the writer would make a connection between the book and the death of his child.

I tend not to be a mystic. I tend not to believe in magic. But it's undeniable that weird things happen in the world all the time, and one has the feeling that books can sometimes provoke these events.

Do I think writing is a dangerous activity? Writing can be very bad for one's mental health. It looks innocent enough from the outside, but when a man or a woman is living every day in an imaginary world, it's often difficult to separate your own reality from the imaginary reality you're writing about. So no, I don't really believe that the book has any magic property. It's simply that Sidney at times believes that it does.


## RUSSELL BANKS

Actually, I have had a toothache as bad as the one Wade had in *Affliction*. I've also had an earache that was as bad as that toothache. But what they share is that it's pain you can't get away from. Pain in other parts of your body, you can isolate. But pain in the head you can't get away from. It was therefore a useful metaphor in the novel *Affliction* for the rage that Wade had repressed.

With regard to *Cloudsplitter*, I researched the period and the life of John Brown and his family for many months before I knew how to enter that world of fiction. And it didn't happen until, at the Rare Book Room in the library at Columbia University, I uncovered the transcripts of interviews made in 1903 with John Brown's surviving children, who had been very young, in fact, too young, in the 1850s, to have been reliable witnesses to those events. His son, Owen Brown, however, was never interviewed. Never wrote a memoir or account. But he had been at his father's side at all the most crucial events. He escaped Harpers Ferry and disappeared into the abolitionist underground, lived out his life as a hermit shepherd, and died in 1889. By authorial fiat, I allowed him to live into the twentieth century and relay his story to his father's biographer, Oswald Garrison Villard. That was my entry point to the novel. Once I knew who was speaking, and to whom, the rest came naturally.

JHUMPA LAHIRI

The proportion of real life and invention really differs from work to work. Sometimes the characters are totally invented, and other times there's a real-life analogue—in the case of "The Third and Final Continent," certainly. But there's really no way to predict how much is drawn from experience and how much is imagined.

With "The Third and Final Continent," the story grew out of an anecdote that my father sometimes told about his arrival in the United States. I was struck by the circumstances of a man coming to a new country in the recent wake of the moon landing, and how that historical event strangely paralleled what this character was experiencing and what my father was experiencing. When my father spoke of that time, he spoke of it very briefly. I only had a few details to work with. According to my father, his landlady, who was 103 years old, was a piano teacher. I made up the detail about her hands hurting. I don't know if that was true. I knew that she couldn't stop talking about the fact that man had landed on the moon. That's all I had. Everything else, I had to build from my own imagination and from my own experiences of coming to a new place and being in a foreign environment and learning to adjust.

CHARLES BAXTER

I suffer from the particular kind of insomnia that allows you to fall asleep but then causes you to wake up in the middle of the night, wide awake. I thought I would put it to use in *The Feast of Love* and set up Charlie Baxter as a sort of sleepless collector-of-stories. That entire book is haunted by moonlight, in any case. Insomnia seemed to fit its contours very nicely.

## COLM TÓIBÍN

I work as a novelist, which means I think in images and scenes. I'm not a biographer, and I'm not a moralist. Therefore, my interest is in the creation of drama. So my interest in Henry James's character for *The Master* was in its dramatic possibilities—what I could do with this, rather than in trying to reconstruct a piece of history. When I was working, I was surrounded with books. I wrote some of the book in Spain and some of it in Dublin, with a duplicate James library that cost me a fortune—two full sets of everything. But sometimes a sentence by him or about him would be enough to get me going, and I could work for three or four pages without looking up.

I didn't base the book on any of his books, but I did pick what I believe were the eleven most dramatic episodes, and I worked on them for all they were worth, and I used as much fact as I could find and that didn't get in my way.

## JOYCE CAROL OATES

For *Blonde*, primarily I did research into the available films of Marilyn Monroe, beginning with her earliest movies and continuing to her final movie, *The Misfits*. I was so very impressed by the quality of her performances, and also, overall, by their diversity. I read two or three biographies and deliberately did not take very many notes, because I wanted to imagine the astonishing person who was Norma Jean Baker, who became concealed in and eventually lost in the iconic image of "Marilyn Monroe." I felt that "Marilyn Monroe" was a performance by a gifted and sometimes desperate young woman. One of my epigraphs is Jean-Paul Sartre's remark that "genius is not a talent, but a way we behave in desperate circumstances." I thought this applied very poignantly to Norma Jean Baker.

## ANDREA LEVY

When I set out to write *Small Island*, the catalyst was my parents' coming to Britain from Jamaica in 1948. There was an event in 1948 where a ship called the *Empire Windrush* sailed from the Caribbean to Britain. On board were about five hundred West Indians or men from the Caribbean who were coming from there to start a new life in Britain. This event caused a great stir at the time. There was talk of having the ship turned back, of not letting these men land. But the ship arrived, and its arrival has come to be seen now in British history, rightly or wrongly, as the point when Britain began to change into a multicultural society. And my dad was on that ship.

So I wanted to look at that immigration. But one thing that I remembered whenever my parents talked about their early days in England was that they always mentioned the white people who took them in. And so from then, I always realized that immigration is a dynamic. It's about the people who came and the people whom they came to. I wanted to look at the whole situation, not just from one point of view.

And so in my book, there are two black narrators from Jamaica, named Hortense and Gilbert, and two white English people, Queenie and Bernard. Hortense and Gilbert come to

live in the house of Queenie Bligh. And the book is about
their meeting, that point of contact. And what happened to
these people before they met in 1948. Queenie's husband,
Bernard, was posted to India with the Royal Air Force, during World War II, and he hadn't returned after the war's end.
Gilbert was in the RAF, too.


## JOHN McNALLY

I don't really begin the stories thinking, Do I know enough
about this? Because it's so much rooted in character. For me,
if I feel comfortable in the voice, it's filtering and processing
things through the consciousness of the character. I always
think I don't write autobiographically, but when people start
dissecting the story—"Where'd you get this?"—it's always
things that are autobiographical, and those things come about
subconsciously. So I can't really separate writing what I know
and writing what I don't know.


## STUART DYBEK

I'm not even sure I write about Chicago. I think I re-imagine
Chicago, and it surprises me when I get e-mails and letters
from people who grew up in the same neighborhood I did
and say, "You really caught it." Because my first allegiance is
to the imagination, and to the way I'm imagining the story.
Most writers write that way.

Whether you're writing about Chicago or whatever your
subject is, I think that with the "writing what you know"
stuff, what you have to remember is that the imagination
doesn't feast on fact. So sometimes, whether it's library work

or life-work research, what you have to keep in mind is you're feeding the imagination. What you know is not what you're writing about. You're using what you know to make imaginative leaps.

You're writing what you know so that you can write what you don't know.

## MARIE ARANA

We were talking the other day about journalists who became novelists because they were afraid that any day they'd slip fiction into what was supposed to be fact. I think Alice McDermott said that once. And so did Gail Godwin.

Yes, the writing is best when you leave all reality behind and go with your imagination. But there's something compelling, too, about constructing a world that people can recognize and learn from.

In writing *Cellophane*, I did so much research about the rain forest. Botanical. The fauna, too. And it was fascinating! I found that maybe I could deliver a world that was there along with the world I was inventing.

## ALICE McDERMOTT

Fiction is not merely a palatable way to get the same information you get from nonfiction. It's the way to enter into another universe, a way to see the world anew, to hear an internal voice that is not your own, to make sense of and to find shape in what (in real life) can often seem senseless and shapeless. People begin reading a novel not with the question of "What's this about?" but rather, "How does this sound?"—

to notice language and image and voice before story and plot. I'm making a pitch here. I have nothing against nonfiction, but fiction is where you'll find the stuff you can't find anywhere else, the stuff that endures—or, as our English teachers used to tell us, the eternal truths.

# 5

## Home Is Where the Art Is

### *How Writers Are Influenced by Place*

James Joyce and Dublin. William Faulkner and Mississippi. Jean Rhys and the Caribbean. Hemingway and Spain.

Writers are often connected with the places they write about—usually, a place where they've grown up or lived. Paul Auster and Brooklyn. Stuart Dybek and Chicago. Thisbe Nissen and Manhattan.

Although readers will complain if a novelist has traffic going west instead of east on West 102nd Street in New York, a writer's evocation of a place is not just about accuracy. Stuart Dybek's Chicago is different from John McNally's Chicago is different from Saul Bellow's Chicago. Place is as individual as what one character will notice when walking into a room as compared to another—and what that same character will notice about the same room at a different moment in the book.

Nor is place the setting of a story only. The Irish immigrant community that populates Alice McDermott's work is not brought to life so much by the physical landscape as it is by the people, the language, the customs. Even the way a writer tells a story may be influenced by place. McDermott's novels unfold in the same way that family secrets are revealed in many Irish-American families—in pieces, the truth revealed bit by bit. Place provides more than a backdrop for a short story or novel. It can make the story what it is.

## ALICE McDERMOTT

As I was growing up, I didn't think there was anything more bland than life on Long Island in a family of Irish Catholics. . . I remember going to Washington for the first time (on an eighth-grade school trip) and thinking, At last— glamour, history, interesting lives. . . .

I suppose I see one of the obligations of fiction as an attempt to discover what, in any bland existence, whether it be in the suburbs or the city, among the rich and famous or the plain and ordinary, is worth recalling, is authentic—what endures.

I write about places as my characters see them (or remember them, which is something else again), not as they really are. This is why I never became a journalist—I couldn't write about a real place or person or event if I tried. I'm always looking to get something other than the literal "truth" out of everything I write about. So it's not my "feel" for a place, it's my character's.

## MARIE ARANA

Someone famous (García Márquez maybe?) said that every-thing he ever wrote about in his novels he knew before the age of eight.

I feel very much the same.

Peru infuses everything I do, because it was where I first

saw daylight and where I learned the hard business of being a small person in a large world. I somehow can't take my head out of Peru, because it seems to me that all the important emotions for me were first felt there.

I go back several times every year. My husband and I have a place in Lima.

But I think that if I never went back, if I were to do all my writing henceforward sitting in Logan Circle in Washington, DC, I'd still be writing about the Andes, the Amazon, that rugged Pacific coast.


MAUREEN HOWARD

I'm from Connecticut, and I've used Connecticut a lot in my work. Indeed, I use it in *The Silver Screen*. I very much wanted Bel, the Murphys, to be somewhat displaced people. And they are somewhat displaced in Rhode Island. It's not home, though they make it home. It's kind of like a new leaf, a place where, given her past and she was recognizably Bel Maher, the actress, it's a way of escaping reality. I also suppose that I visited Rhode Island, where my daughter and family go often in the summer, and could see the possibility of the sea and how that would tie in with Melville. Whereas the industrial river towns of Connecticut don't quite do that for me. I didn't have a particular town in mind to name. I could point to it on a map but I didn't want to give it a name. The actual place would be quite different now.


THISBE NISSEN

*Osprey Island* is definitely influenced and shaped by summers and weekends spent on Shelter Island, on the tip of Long

Island, between the North and South Forks. And I think my
draw toward that setting is there because I have such a visceral memory of that place and the time I spent there as a
kid. The quality of air and light is unique. And I don't live in
a place like that at all now. And I really do think I write in
some cases to evoke those feelings in myself, to awaken that
visceral sense of a place. It's like going on a little private
vacation.

I think the small town-ness of *Osprey Island* was almost
inbred into what that island is to me. When I was workshop-
ping a very early draft of this, someone called the island a perfect petri dish. The small community of this island is the
perfect place for things to germinate and grow. The closeness
of it all was sort of exciting to me, and that's what drove it.

I feel like when I was writing *Out of the Girls' Room and
into the Night* and *Good People of New York*, I was definitely
processing through my experiences of having lived for eighteen years in an urban center—not to say that I've processed
through all of that at all. But now, having lived in the
Midwest pretty much since I left for college in 1990, the
things I'm taking in on a regular basis have much more to do
with small towns than big cities. Certainly, in every city and
every neighborhood the pockets get smaller and each certainly does have its own tone. But it feels different to me. I
wonder if it's just the tenor of it that feels different. I have sort
of written it off to making sense of my life in New York, and
now the things around me are small town, and it's what I'm
taking in and processing through. In a way, while there is the
element of my time in New York in *Osprey Island,* my interest is very much with the locals. Choosing to set the novel
before the summer people showed up was important. I was
interested in the people out there who are a lot more like the

people around me, who in turn are like the people around me now in Iowa City.

## JOYCE CAROL OATES

I'm drawn to write about upstate New York in the way in which a dreamer might have recurring dreams. My childhood and girlhood were spent in upstate New York, in the country north of Buffalo and west of Rochester. So this part of New York state is very familiar to me and, with its economic difficulties, has become emblematic of much of American life. I've only written one novel set in Rochester, *The Tattooed Girl*.

## PAUL AUSTER

I wrote before I ever moved to Brooklyn, and I've continued to write ever since I've been here, which is now almost twenty-four years. It's my place. It's this little spot on earth that I inhabit. And because I'm surrounded by it every day, it's only natural that I'd want to write about it at times.

## STUART DYBEK

Sure, there's a Chicago style or Chicago aesthetic. Do writers pay attention to it is maybe another question. Consciously, I'd have to say no. But I think that any writer of place is just kind of wired to express both the physical landscape and whatever psychological landscape all places carry with them.

We could talk about Chicago writers and group them with urban writers, or writers of place. And you'll see that writers writing about Chicago have a lot in common with

Eudora Welty writing about Mississippi, or James Joyce writing about Dublin. So these categories always come after the creative work. I wrote an essay for a book called *Chicago Stories*, and I tried to pick out things that typify Chicago writers, but I wasn't doing that as a writer; I was doing it as a reader. As a reader you draw conclusions, and it's a certain kind of thinking that universities are fond of, but it's different from writing. For me, what would typify Chicago writers is an interest in neighborhood, and in immigration, and in ethnicity. This is a city where everyone asks you, "What are you?" The answer is never "American."

I think one of the things that does in fact typify Chicago writers is an interest in sentiment—they write work that asks the reader to feel something. There isn't that ironical detachment. This is one of the few cities in the United States where class is an open consideration in the work. Class is an American something that you're absolutely taught not to think about. You can think about race, gender, ethnicity, but you can't think about class. That's not true in Chicago.

JOHN McNALLY

I think Chicago does have its own literary aesthetic, but I'm not sure how to define it because I think it varies from author to author. But I think it's like the people in Chicago—I mean, most of the people I knew growing up were working class. I think of Chicago as a working-class city, and most of the fiction I think of has that kind of backdrop to it. It seems to be informed by work, by what people do. But beyond that, it's hard for me really to define it. In some ways, when I think of New York fiction I think of its being kind of coy perhaps, and self-consciously ironic. When I think of Chicago fiction, I think of it as gritty, and when humorous, it might be more of a smart-ass humor than coy.

I'm not consciously trying to write a Chicago style. But since I grew up here, it's just part of my sensibility. I wasn't able to write about it right after I moved away. It took me about ten years or so. I've lived here one year since 1983, and I find myself writing more and more about Chicago. But I'm not consciously trying to adopt a certain kind of city or urban Chicago style.

## MARGOT LIVESEY

I did read Scottish folktales when writing *Eva Moves the Furniture*, but I had also grown up on Scottish folktales, so many of them were already embedded in my memory and in my way of looking at life. And the Scottish folktales were present not only in books but also in the landscape of my childhood. On the way to school every day, I passed the grave of the legendary Scottish poet Ossian, a Roman encampment, and a place where a dairymaid had drowned in the river and was meant to walk at harvest time. All of this fueled my imagination when writing *Eva Moves the Furniture*.

Certainly living between two countries has changed my approach to fiction. I first came to Boston in 1983, and although I still go back to Britain frequently, I haven't lived there continuously for quite a long time. I think one of the most significant advantages of this back-and-forth is that it enables me to see what I previously took for granted in Britain with a much sharper eye. People and situations that previously would have seemed too ordinary to play a role in fiction, seem extraordinarily interesting from a distance of 2,300 miles. I would also add that I'm aware of the gaps in my knowledge of British life, so I work very assiduously doing research while I write my novels and have British friends read my work to make sure I am keeping abreast of the many changes in the culture.

So far, my main characters have all been British, but I'm imagining as time goes on that American characters will begin to play a larger role in my fiction.

## ANDREA LEVY

*Small Island*, the title, refers to Britain and to Jamaica, and it also refers to the people. During World War II, it became clear to people in Britain that they were a small island—at that time, the empire was starting to shrink back to its center, which is Britain. Instead of being a nation that colored the world pink with all the lands that it owned, the empire started to crumble and shrink. So that's the British part.

As for the Jamaican part, in the Caribbean, the term *small island* is used for all the other islands that are not Jamaica. In the Caribbean, Jamaica is a big island, and it was rather disparaging to call someone a "small islander." So the Jamaicans grew up with the notion of living on the bigger island. During World War II again, a lot of the men left for Europe to fight and for America to work, and when they returned, they returned to what felt like a very small place.

Also, *Small Island* refers to the book's four narrators, who are all telling their tales from their own perspectives. You've got four narrators who are small islands in themselves— they're just telling their tales.

GISH JEN

There's no question that without my trips to China, there would be no books. For one thing, I certainly could not have written the character of Lan in *The Love Wife* without first-hand knowledge of contemporary Chinese and how they think.

DOREEN BAINGANA

Uganda has been central to most of the stories I have written, especially those in *Tropical Fish: Stories Out of Entebbe*. But it will not always figure in my work—at least I hope not. I don't want to restrict myself to any one place, subject matter, or anything else. I started off writing fantasy fiction, where I created imagined spaces that mostly turned out to be different forms of Eden, followed by the fall. But even when one writes about real places, one re-creates them using words rather than soil. The place on the page cannot be an exact replica of the geographical space—also because the writer uses this detail and omits that to serve a particular end, such as to evoke mood or reveal character.

Paradoxically, the real places one writes about keep changing over time, but published words don't; they fix in place particular settings at particular points in time.

I have set stories in Uganda, and Entebbe in particular, because this is what I know best, having spent the first twenty-three years of my life there. Second, I wrote those stories partly as an act of nostalgia. Away from Uganda, in the United States, I tried to recapture places that had once been so familiar that I didn't really see them then, but once I left,

I kept journeying back in dreams and daydreams, and even more so in writing. The writing process itself expanded and deepened my memories because I had to dig up and describe physical and other details beyond mere impressions. That process was immensely pleasurable. Now, what I have written seems more real to me than my memories.

I am particularly interested in telling stories set on the African continent, as opposed to stories "about Africa," which is such a simplification that it is false, and as absurd as stories "about Europe." Stories set in contemporary urban spaces about all sorts of Africans whose influences, welcomed or not, are global, have not been told enough. The Western world's wild, picturesque, or poverty-ridden view of Africa is old and tired. So is the expatriate *Out of Africa* story that Western publishers can't seem to get over. Because I wrote my stories in the West, where this simplistic view dominates and often contradicts my own experience, I wrote partly to counter that monolithic impression of Africa. This may not be an appropriately artistic impulse; perhaps I should not care what else is written about Africa, but I do. Fiction is a great vehicle for the exploration and revelation of the myriad complexities of any given situation. I also was deliberately specific in my subtitle, *Stories Out of Entebbe*, but I fear it appears to be merely derivative, not oppositional. The irony is lost.

## RUSSELL BANKS

In July 2003, as I was finishing *The Darling,* I tried to get into Liberia, just as it erupted into violence again. The roads were closed by the warlords and people were being kidnapped and killed, and as a husband, a son, and the father of four daughters, I decided that the better part of valor was to stay in Sierra Leone, where it was only marginally calmer.

Was it disappointing not to be able to go? Yes and no. I was there as a novelist, not as a journalist or a historian, so I was interested in the sound, smell, and look of the place, its physical presence. And Sierra Leone, which is adjacent to Liberia and has a similar history, gave me enough information that I felt confident in writing about Liberia.


TIM PARKS

It seems to me that only one place is really home. I remember very distinctly about twelve years ago, the time when I really felt that the center of my life had finally shifted from England to Italy. I was in London for work and I just kept thinking, I should really be back home, in Verona. Obviously, the change of language, the business of absorbing another culture and its literature, and then all the translation I've done from Italian to English has radically changed the person I am and the work I do. I don't really feel I'm an English novelist anchored in the English tradition. There's something more. And this has been one of my great fortunes in life. In particular, it seems to me that the new language and the work with translation make you hyper-aware of how much of literature is driven and partly created by the language in which it's written and by the community of people who speak that language. So what tends to get lost in translation is the author's personal use of the language he's using. For example, if D. H. Lawrence says, "She was destroyed into perfect consciousness," then the reader is aware not just of the strange statement but also of the way it is in an abrasive relationship with a standard English use. Anyway, the more you become sensi-

tive to this kind of thing, the more humble you feel about
your own individuality but also the more excited about the
possibilities of working within and sometimes against the
common language.

E. L. DOCTOROW

The "sweet land" in *Sweet Land Stories* is, of course, the
United States. As in "My country 'tis of thee, sweet land of
liberty"—which means, for many of us, the liberty to make a
mess of our lives.

# 6

# All That Jazz

## *Playing with Language and*
## *Style to Suit the Story*

Here is the fun stuff of writing—words, sentences, phrases, structure, image, voice. It is the matter of which writing consists, like clay for a sculptor. Time to play. As writers talk about finding a style for their stories, they sound like painters talking about color, or a child fingerpainting. This sound, this rhythm, this type of voice, this mood, this concept to tie it all together.

How much of style is innate, how much practiced? Surely, Michael Cunningham wrote *The Hours* in the way he did because he is Michael Cunningham. As in everything else in writing, it's both. Style is also an exploration. What is right for this story, this character, this scene, this moment within this scene? Writers talk about the influences on their writing—Stuart Dybek breathes in Miles Davis, Michael Cunningham analyzes Virginia Woolf, Maureen Howard looks at V. S. Naipaul—and how they both use and move away from those influences, take what they need and then find their own way.

Oh, new book? Time to start all over again. No one wants to get stale.

As one hears writers talk about style, what remains astonishing is how inevitable a style seems once an author succeeds in creating it. How, when it's right, the style is the book (is the character is the theme is the story is the writer). How it all fits together.

## MICHAEL CUNNINGHAM

In an earlier draft of *The Hours*, the correspondences between Woolf's characters and mine were more direct. I tried to more thoroughly incorporate *Mrs. Dalloway* into my book. And when I looked at what I had, it felt a little lifeless. It had a certain precision that was more like a Swiss music box than a novel.

I went back and read *Mrs. Dalloway* again and was reminded that part of what I love about that novel is its looseness, its riff-ish quality. The way it reads almost like a jazz musician playing improvisations. It has loose ends, it has stray threads. And I decided it would be more appropriate, it would be a better tribute to *Mrs. Dalloway*, if I loosened up my own book, if I didn't insist on such strict parallels, if I injected into *The Hours* a rough correspondence to *Mrs. Dalloway* and didn't insist upon making it so precise.

## TIM PARKS

I'm constantly trying to vary what I do and the approach I take. At the most obvious level, I try to alternate between, say, an intense novel and then a piece of lighter nonfiction, *A Season with Verona*, for example, or a book of essays. (Actually, I've just finished *Medici Money*, a short history book about the Medici bank in the fifteenth century.) Then, within the novels, I'm constantly looking for a different style, a different kind of voice. Usually I'll do two in the same sort of voice—*Europa* and *Destiny* maybe—then change. It seems important to keep unsettling myself, to go right back to square one, to ask myself, How do you write a book? Otherwise I'll get stale. That said, there is always a continuity of vision, of attitude to life. In fact, it's that continuity that makes the approach–change necessary.

As for the dialogue in *Judge Savage*, the whole effort of the recent books has been to create a very fluid voice that may be inside or outside the character's head, in the past or the present, without particular markers or indicators, so that the reader is always on his toes. Nothing is reassuring.

I had to work and work and work at it, and I often spend hours seeing what happens to a piece of prose if you introduce into it a fragment from elsewhere, and how you can establish a rhythm of such introductions. But there's nothing Joycean about it. He tried to bring in sensation and a sort of lyricism, as if the mind were constantly creating poetry. This has much more to do with the obsessive voice in the head.

## RICHARD FORD

Voice to me is at best a poorly understood term. What voice means to me is the music of a story's intelligence, and that music is composed of the rhythms of the sentences, the length of the sentences, how much the sentences stress the reader's intelligence, the rhythms of the whole book, the length of the whole book, how many "-ly" adverbs there are, how many adjectives, how many active verbs, and certainly over the course of twenty years of writing Frank Bascombe, that music has changed.

## THISBE NISSEN

When I started *Osprey Island*, I was probably mostly doing what I often do when I'm writing, which is write myself back into a place that I used to know or want to revisit in myself. If I had to name a book that I had in mind, I spent a lot of time in the beginning thinking about John Irving's *The Cider House Rules*, which fascinated me because of its point of view, which was in a lot of ways what I was wanting to tackle in this novel. Irving has an amazing ability, a real dexterity, in that novel in particular, where he is able to create a narrative voice that is a very omniscient third person who hovers above the world and can see with enormous scope, while at the same time is able to swoop down almost into the minds of major and minor characters alike, and then swoop back up. I had never tried something like that. And point of view has always been my obsession and my albatross, I think. I read *The Cider House Rules* and thought, How does he do that? I want to figure out how to do that! In the end, I ended up doing nothing close to what he did, but it led me on my own path.

## ART SPIEGELMAN

I tried to keep *Maus* very humble, and I actually struggled for a long time to find a drawing style appropriate to it. I tend to be a stylistic switch-hitter, and my first stabs were kind of like Eastern European wood engravings for children's books. I found the tone all wrong. It's as if I was saying, "I can sort of draw and you can't, so shut up and listen." What I finally opted for was something actually equally arduous: drawing that could look like a kind of handwriting, like a visual journal entry, drawn the same size it was printed, to make it more intimate. Nevertheless, in the second volume, *Maus II*, the success of the first volume weighed me down enough so that I had to include a sequence about the unseemliness of the first book's success, a picture of me at my drawing table perched on top of a mountain of dead bodies, with journalists scrambling up the side to interview me. (Those pages allowed me to continue with my project but required close to a year of therapy to draw.)

Comics is the language I speak the most fluently, despite how slowly I work. And cartoonists often are punished for being able to both write and draw, rather than doing both together, which is ten times harder. I certainly don't think of *In the Shadow of No Towers* as a graphic novel—more like a graphic novelty. What else could you call ten giant-size plates in baby board book format? I guess *Maus* qualifies for "graphic novel" status even if it is nonfiction. I made it after having a vision of a very fat comic book that needed a bookmark. *In the Shadow of No Towers* is a very different animal than *Maus*, something that some reviewers have complained about bitterly, but I couldn't make *Maus III* (World War II had ended), and I never even knew that these *No Towers* pages I was making while waiting for the world to end—just to keep my hands busy—would even be a book.


JOANNA SCOTT

In my first two books I was very close to my main characters, stuck inside their heads. And then, with *Arrogance,* I broke the narrative into different voices. I introduced many different characters, and that helped me to develop a confidence to move in a more flexible fashion among different parts of a story.

But once I wrote *Arrogance*, I was done with that form. I don't want to repeat myself. I'm just getting close to finishing up a new novel right now, and it feels like, That's it. I'm done. I'll never write another book. And the only way I can write another book is to tell myself, "I'm going to do something different." Even as I'm learning from what I'm writing, I have to leave the work behind and start from scratch. I want to keep trying out new things, new forms, learn something I didn't know before.


## MAUREEN HOWARD

The structure of a novel never loses its interest for me. I'm obviously not attracted too often to straight linear narrative. I think that the idea of memory, the memory of my characters—memory calls up so much and contains so much of life for them and for us, and it connects to imagination, so that you imagine so much that you think you remember exactly, yet you are constantly making up the past, and the past is constantly intruding on the present. And so I find that I have different places that I go to when I'm writing. For instance, it's the priest who can't get over the fact that he does not have a deeply spiritual life. And so he tries to connect to the exercises of Ignatius Loyola. I hope people will find it funny. This poor guy is trying to live on a scale of high-flown belief, and he goes back to family stories. He just can't make it to that pure place of contemplation. His head is full of fragments of poetry that he thought would do the spiritual thing for him. Even poor Rita is displaced in California—she keeps thinking of the man who fit her shoe and the man who worked at home. This free, beautiful life is cluttered with sadness and memories of the past.

I like a number of different voices, and different voices can bring me to different places. I do not mind an intrusive voice on my part. I'm not at all shy about that. The nineteenth-century novelists—George Eliot could easily do a gloss on politically where she was. I'm talking about an authorial voice coming in. That gives the writer a lot of freedom. I don't think it's all that old-fashioned. I'm thinking of Javier Marias, who uses himself all the way through. Naipaul, all of them. They're telling a story.

## RUSSELL BANKS

I was trying to obtain an intimacy and a personalized narrative voice that was not eccentric or calling attention to itself in any obvious way. And I suppose in some sense, that is a convention of the nineteenth century. Those writers are ambitious inasmuch as they try to concern the larger world rather than the purely domestic world. They try to conjoin the personal and the public, and the private with the historical, so I guess they are large in that sense. But whether or not they actually succeed in attaining that ambition, I can't say.

## MARGOT LIVESEY

I think in *Eva Moves the Furniture*, the two companions were central to my aim in writing the novel and in dramatizing the way in which Eva is both blessed and isolated by her unique relationship with what we might call the supernatural. As for striking a balance between the mythical and the realistic, that's something I very much aspire to do, and I think several of my works have been based on very old stories. In *Criminals*, I returned to the image of finding a baby or a changeling, and in *Banishing Verona*, I'm very much following in the footsteps of the many authors who have written novels of quests or pilgrimages, whether for romantic love or some other aim.

## JOYCE CAROL OATES

Writers generally reflect their society and their time. Stendhal spoke of the novel as a mirror moving along a roadway, and this is an excellent image for the realistic novel. It doesn't, of course, reflect the interior of our lives, our psychological and spiritual lives. But another kind of fiction, a more psychologically analytical fiction, can express that life. The tradition in which I see myself is that of psychological realism, which attempts to mirror the complex outside world of society, politics, art, domestic life, as well as to interpret it. In my longer novels, especially, I do a fair amount of research, and often I learn much that I didn't realize I did not know, as in my novel *The Falls*, which takes place in Niagara Falls, about fifteen miles from where I grew up. It brought me to a historical knowledge of that city and its region that I had not known.

## DOREEN BAINGANA

Because most of my education has been in English, I think my writing tradition is Western, unfortunately. I wrote *Tropical Fish* when I was getting an MFA at the University of Maryland, so I was following the format of a classic short story, which is Western. So I would like to believe that, having grown up in Africa, I am influenced by the African tradition, perhaps not consciously as such. Perhaps I am more interested in approaching the subject matter in a new way. Most of what we hear and read about Africa is negative, so in that sense, I'm trying to highlight the positives, such as the closeness of families, and how people deal with political chaos around them and still create a somewhat normal life. And I try to show that perhaps the struggle that people go through in daily life is similar to what people in the West go through. So in terms of content, I'd like to have an approach to African material that is not what you see in the media. Perhaps what exactly is an African tradition is also contested.

## TOD GOLDBERG

It's an odd thing. I'm not a huge fan of surreal fiction, and when I think about the writing I do, I see myself as being very tangible and tactile, yet I go back and read my work and there's Elvis bleeding on the wall. It's not a response to pop culture as much as it is a response to how people cope, or fail to cope. I remember clearly as a child drifting off to another place when things got scary at home, or when people were yelling at each other, and I suspect that the way I end up writing these stories is a response to that. I think of writers such as Aimee Bender, who I think is the finest practitioner of magic realism America has, and I don't see bizarre or odd happenings, I see people struggling to stay afloat.

Stories typically present themselves to me in the first person. When I wrote my first novel, *Fake Liar Cheat*, and my second, *Living Dead Girl*, I wanted to write both of them from the point of view of an unreliable narrator, and that meant first person was the most likely voice, and probably the most successful choice as well. And, as is often the case with my short stories, I tend to see things first through the eyes of a person, and for that reason I guess first person has always compelled me (plus I have an enormous ego). But when I wrote the story "Rise John Wayne and Rebuke Them" for the collection in the third person, I felt a real sense of freedom that first person hadn't supplied me with in years. It was like getting behind the wheel of a BMW after a lifetime spent rollin' deep in a Tercel. So, I suspect that I will return to third more often now. I was scared of it before and now it feels safe.


MARIE ARANA

*Cellophane* was written against the category of magical realism. And yet, as fate would have it, all the critics have said, "Isn't this wonderful? It's magical realism all over again!"

The butterflies-in-the-hat business actually happened to the grandfather of a friend of mine. He collected the butterflies in his hat and then pulled it off when he proposed marriage to my friend's grandmother. And yet reviews of *Cellophane* said, "You know when you're in that butterfly/hat scene that you're in magical realism territory!"

Nothing in *Cellophane* happens that couldn't happen in this hard, real world of ours. It's that characters in the book *believe* magic is happening. And that is the whole message.

Okay. I'll have out with it now: I *hate* the term *magical realism*.

There's no such thing. It's a convenient label (condescending, actually) that's put on a lot of writing about South America. It's as if someone in South America decided that all writing in English was "domestic realism"—all that Jane

Austen! Michael Cunningham! Anne Tyler!—going on endlessly about the quotidian details of family!

Latins believe in magic. Our mythologies teach us to. It isn't a literary conceit.

So, no, I don't write magical realism. Neither does García Márquez. Or Isabel Allende. South Americans write what they know.

End of rant.

But yes, as you say, there have been many very interesting books recently that employ plot devices that couldn't possibly happen—narration by a dead person (*The Lovely Bones*), for instance. I don't think of these as magical realism. I simply think of them as mythical explorations. Humankind has been doing that for a long time.

GISH JEN

I don't have any tricks for making a book funny. For whatever reason, the humor seems a genetic trait from which I could not escape if I wanted to. I do worry sometimes that I am too funny, and in the editing process, I'm often working to bring out other tones, because the humor can be like a bright light that blanches out everything else.

PAUL AUSTER

Life is both funny and not funny. It has its tragic moments and its hilarious moments. I try in my work to embrace all aspects of what it means to be alive, and humor is an important part of that. So even in some of my grimmest works, there have been comic touches. There have to be, because that's the way we're built as human beings, and often when we're in dark circumstances, we survive them by cracking jokes.

Humor is eternal. Comedy is eternal. And no matter what the circumstances of a particular moment, there are always going to be people making jokes about what is happening. Styles of humor change over the years, but to say that humor in general would die would be like saying the human race is going to die.

## MARTIN AMIS

Satire has been called "militant irony." This suggests that you're actually trying to change things. I don't feel I am, except in the broader sense of trying to enrich the imaginations of my readers. . . . I'd like to be remembered as someone who kept the comic novel going for another generation or so. I fear the comic novel is in retreat. A joke is by definition politically incorrect—it assumes a butt, and a certain superiority in the teller. The culture won't put up with that for much longer.

I only try to "sound American" when I have an American narrator. But my connections with America are so deep and lifelong that the more demotic rhythms of the American language are to be found in mine. And certainly, I have always been a reader of American literature, rather than my native brand: It's something to do with hitting various registers at the same time, and not sticking to a middling, bourgeois kind of voice.

## STUART DYBEK

We're in the twenty-first century, and the twentieth century was a century of hybrid form, and to have some ignoring the fact that there are prose poems, and hybrid forms, and not admitting hybrid forms become their own forms, seems odd. It's not like we haven't had *Winesburg, Ohio* around, and *Dubliners*, for a while. They're seminal in contemporary literature. Those are books that I really like a lot, and some of them have been the most important books in my life.

When you write your own version of a book like that, it's got to be in some sense an homage. Almost everything Italo Calvino writes is in that form. His models were Chaucer, Boccaccio. So books like this go way back.

The other things I grew up with were *Kind of Blue, Sketches of Spain, Sgt. Pepper's Lonely Hearts Club Band*. Maybe as a prose writer I can put this kind of concept book together. What it invites is an enormous collaboration between the writer and the reader. You're asking the reader to participate, but you're telling the reader there are all sorts of clues here. Just like the painters who do sequences. Does Goya see those sequences beforehand in *The Disasters of War?* The writer is participating, is seeing the sequential qualities, and the reader then participates in seeing the sequential qualities, the way you don't do with *The Brothers Karamazov.*

I like that looseness enormously, and it goes back to poetry in a way, because that's how poets put together a collection, and sometimes they write poems they wouldn't have written if they hadn't gotten involved in sequence.

# 7

# The Long and Short of It

## *The Differences Between Writing Novels and Writing Short Stories*

It has been said that writing a short story is like going out to sea in a small boat and hugging the shore, and writing a novel is like going out to sea and rowing until you can't see the shore. Each has its dangers; each has its thrills.

Some authors will only be short-story writers (Alice Munro, for example); others are only novelists (George Eliot). But how do the writers who travel between the two navigate these waters?

The first response this question seems to generate is metaphor—six popped up in the comments included here, in addition to the one I've used. Dating and marriage, marriage and affairs, houses and rooms, rooms and closets . . . they all relate to the length of time that one needs to write a story versus a novel, the depth of character and story that each must include, the precision needed for the shorter form, the sins more easily forgiven in a novel.

And then even more metaphors come to mind. Are novels, as Henry James once called them, "loose, baggy monsters"? The precision of *The Hours* belies that. Walter Mosley gets at the falseness of these concepts as well in the quote that begins this chapter. A good short story is not in any way shallow or quick. It has its own depths. They just aren't necessarily present on the page.

## WALTER MOSLEY

I think of novels as mountains, and short stories as far-flung islands that are the tips of mountains. The idea is that poetry and short stories are very crystalline. Each word, each idea, each movement is specific and unalterable. Whereas in novel writing, as E. M. Forster says, "It's 50,000 words more or less of spongy prose." And so, when writing a short story, you have to know everything behind it—everything that led up to there, everything about those characters. But you don't have the leisure to talk about it at length. You only see that very upper tip, as with an island compared to the mountain that lies underneath it.

Writing a novel is more difficult than writing a short story, because of the length, but it's less difficult because of the leisure and the language.

## THISBE NISSEN

I think short stories and novels serve very different drives in me. I like getting wrapped up in a novel, and the particular kinds of challenges and problems that you have to solve working on a novel, and the research one has to do working on a novel. I love doing that. And the latitude to follow whims and funny trails and see where they lead you is a lot greater in a novel. On the other hand, I enjoy the economy of short stories and the way it makes my brain have to work to hone ideas into that economized framework.

*Osprey Island* is the first thing I've written that germinated as a novel. It did not start as a short story. The idea came with me fully recognizing it as a novel, as a whole piece. And I wanted to tackle something big. I think I thought this novel was going to be a lot bigger than it was. Even my page counts were less than I thought. It was about 450 manuscript pages, and I thought it was going to be huge, and it turned into another 300-page novel just like the last one.

It was about the desire to evoke that place and time, and the desire to take on the point-of-view challenge, that really drove the novel.

## CHARLES BAXTER

I learned how to write fiction by writing stories. The short-story form is so concentrated, so unforgiving toward mistakes, that when I made a mistake while writing a story, I knew it almost instantly. That's often not the case—it wasn't the case with me—in writing novels. I wrote three unpublished novels that were rather bad, though I didn't realize how bad, or why, until long after I had finished them. For that reason, I feel quite at home writing short stories but nervous and anxious when writing novels, as if that bad time of consecutive failures might arise again.

## MARY KAY ZURAVLEFF

I wrote short stories for years. I love short stories, and I could work in that tight logical construction. Ultimately, I had a few stories going at once, and it occurred to me that if I braided them, as it were, I might have the complications necessary for a novel, which I hadn't thought I could write.

## ELIZABETH GRAVER

When I started out, I thought I was essentially a short-story writer who would "try" a novel, partly because that seemed the thing to do after you'd done a book of short stories (more publishable, etc.), and partly because I was drawn to the challenge of the form. I thought that my attention to inner life and image, along with the fact that I am not, as a writer, particularly plot-driven, would make the novel an awkward form for me, a real stretch.

But it turns out that I love writing novels. I love the way they are always there, for years and years; how the characters stay with you; how they deepen and grow as the book gets more layered. I love how you don't have to reinvent the world each time, how your mind can drift back to the novel at any moment; how, when I am in deep work on a novel, I find connections to it everywhere I look. I love, too, how novels can follow their people over time and thus have a wider, deeper scope (though some stories manage to do this too—the way, for example, Alice Munro leapfrogs through time). I love writing stories too, but they often arrive as unexpected little gifts, written fast and without a lot of revision, and their characters don't stay with me as long. I will always do both, I think, and I am in fact working on a short-story collection now and having a wonderful time. So while I may have initially been prodded toward novels partly because of marketplace concerns, I ended up finding the novel to be a form I genuinely loved.

## JOAN SILBER

I started as a novelist, I did things sort of backward. And one thing I didn't like about short stories is that they focused on one scene. So I wanted to do things that focused on a longer time span. And it was really Alice Munro who showed me the way. Her stories make those great leaps through time. I had to learn how to do it, I had to teach myself how to do it. But I'm not sure I found it harder than doing anything else.

## ALICE McDERMOTT

Publishing a short story can sometimes feel like shouting into the dark . . . your words come out, and then nothing . . . but I don't think that's why I tend to write novels rather than stories. I just like the elbow room a novel gives you—a chance to work out implications over time and space. I also like the puzzle of structure. Very early in my writing life, I wanted to write plays (until I realized I couldn't write, direct, and perform them alone—I'm not one for collaborating), and the novel's structure is more like a play's than a short story's. I do believe a good short story is more difficult to write, however (and a good poem is more difficult still), and I do aim to get some of the short story's more pressing demands into my novels—which may be why they tend to be short.

## DAN CHAON

I am still writing stories, but switching back and forth is very difficult, because to me the process of writing a novel versus writing a short story is a completely different mental process. Part of that has to do with the degree of spontaneity. With a story, I tend to write more subconsciously without knowing the ending and where things are going. With a novel, I think I'm more aware of the architecture of plot and structure. I don't really like one better than the other. I guess it's like the difference between being married and dating. With a story, there's the thrill of discovery, you're in and you're out and you're gone. With a novel, it's a long process of getting to know one another and learning to live with one another. In terms of whether I'm better at one than the other, I don't really know and I guess I can't make that judgment myself. I guess I'll see if I make it through the reviews alive.

It took about two years to write the novel *You Remind Me of Me.* There were some elements that were there beforehand. I was working with some stuff I had already written. One of the dictums of short-story writing is to start in the middle of action, and I tried to do that with the novel. And then I found myself swamped with layers upon layers of flashback and summary. And the only way I could figure out how to handle that thirty years of time was to break it up into fragments and arrange the fragments in a way that showed their interrelationship.

The middle part of the book took the longest for me to write, because I kept changing my mind about what was going to happen. The more I got to know the characters, the more I found they didn't necessarily want to do what I thought they were going to do. I had to backtrack and redo things again. I talked about spontaneity, and the spontaneity in the novel is more lumbering, because turning a novel is sort of like turning the *Titanic.* But those surprises can come.

Ultimately, I think I ended up inventing a somewhat modified rather than classical version of the novel form, particularly in the way that I dealt with chronology. *You Remind Me of Me* is definitely a short-story writer's novel, I would say.

## ANDREA LEVY

I have written short stories—not very many, maybe five. I find them more akin to a poem than a novel, because they're so short and tight. So I enjoy writing them but they take an enormous amount of time for me. Ten pages of a novel would not take me nearly as long as ten pages of a short story. People will say, "Can't you just knock off a short story?" and I just look at them. I need the time to write a short story. And I can't do the two at once.

## FRANCES ITANI

I have written ten books, but *Deafening* was my first novel. The book before *Deafening* is called *Leaning, Leaning Over Water*, and that is a collection of linked stories, so I consider *Leaning* my crossover book. And that really helped me when I began *Deafening* as a novel. There was no question in my mind from the beginning that *Deafening* would be a novel.

But this is a very different form from the short story, which I had been writing for decades. The short story is a very tight, exact genre, and it doesn't have the broad scope of the novel. But it is a huge challenge to ensure that every word in a short story attaches to theme. In some ways, the short story is my favorite genre to write, and I'm working on stories right now, but my next book is going to be a novel, and I have to say that I'm really excited at the thought of getting back into the larger work again.

## E. L. DOCTOROW

I've always found the classic form of the modern short story constrictive. It calls for an entry point close to the dénouement, and turns on a moment of revelation or, as Joyce says, an epiphany. A few years ago, I was asked to edit an anthology of short fiction and to choose, from 150 stories, about twenty. You read them blind and you don't know who wrote them or where they appeared. And the stories I chose, as I was to discover, were often those of first-generation Americans or newly arrived writers from Latin America, the Caribbean, and elsewhere. They were not writing to the classic form. Their stories had more extension to them, and harked back to the tales of the nineteenth century. And that apparently had the subconscious effect of recalling me to my early reading and a renewed appreciation of the old form of the tale. And the result is this volume of *Sweet Land Stories*.

## ANTHONY DOERR

Short stories are wonderful and extremely challenging, and the joy of them—because it only takes me three or four months to write—is that I can take more risks with them. It's just less of your life invested. That's great. But the challenge of a novel is so rewarding—there's so much more you can cram into them. Maybe the metaphor is: With a short story, you're building a table, you have four legs, you're trying to make it as beautiful but as functional as you can. With a novel, you're building not just a table but a whole house—you're building all the furniture inside it. It's more challenging, and then when you finish, it's more rewarding. I do think it's a richer experience.

## HANNAH TINTI

I am working on a novel. I'm about three-quarters of the way through. It's a historical novel about a gang of grave robbers. I'm having a lot of fun with it. It's very interesting to switch forms. This is my first time writing a novel. There's so much more space. There's so much more room to explore these side alleys and side stories that you just can't do with a short story. With a short story, everything has to be on track with your goal. With a novel, I can go off with a side character and tell their story. And I'm having a lot of fun doing that. I think it was Alice Munro who said that a novel is a house with many rooms, and if that's the case, I'd say a short story is a closet—with lots of interesting things in it, but still a closet.

## TOBIAS WOLFF

The shift from stories to a novel wasn't really as great a leap as you might think. In order to write my two memoirs, I had to sustain a narrative over the length of a book, with a limited set of characters and concerns—in other words, both to focus and to expand. This novel, *Old School*, had been brewing for several years before I began to write it. There was never really any question of writing it as a short story. The longer arc of the narrative, the number of people involved, the issues at stake would have burst the seams of a story.

Certainly there's a great difference between the writing of a story and a novel. When you write a story, you can at least assure yourself with some degree of confidence that you will live to finish it. I didn't always have that feeling when I was writing this novel. But over the four years I worked on it, I did come to appreciate the experience of returning to the same world and the same people, entering more and more deeply into their lives, and trying to find the form and tone that would best express those lives. Now when you work on a short story, you're likely to bring it to a conclusion in, say, two and a half or three months—at least that's the case with me—then you have to invent a whole new set of circumstances and call a new set of people to life and try to figure out what's at the heart of their story, what's driving it. You're starting life all over again every three months or so when you're writing short stories, and that can be both exciting and exhausting. So each of the forms has its own compensations and difficulties.

## GISH JEN

I love the novel, I have to say. It's the difference between having an affair and being married. The story is fun because you can go anywhere, you can write about anything. I think in my stories you can see that there's a slightly giddy air to them. I think you can see I'm on holiday. But there's a way in which you can put everything that you know as a human, including the texture of your life, into a novel.

It's the fact that you can be done in a reasonable amount of time. I spent five years on *The Love Wife*. In a short story, the end is in sight. With a novel, the end is never in sight.

I don't think I could write novels without writing stories. Inevitably, over the course of writing a novel, one develops side interests that are better kept out of one's novel. You can pursue your little side interests via the story, and that enables you to save your novel from them. It's a little like having affairs in order to save your marriage. I don't know how well that works in life, but in the context of writing, there is something to be said for it.

# 8

# Lovers and Other Strangers

## *Sex and Love in Literature*

One of the most beguiling aspects of fiction is the sense the reader gets of being inside another person's head. Hearing his thoughts, feeling his emotions. Finding out the difference between what someone thinks and what he says. We can see what characters see, and sometimes we can see what they don't see. Fiction is most alive to me when a writer successfully creates the world of another person—the world we see through his eyes, the world within him.

Is it surprising, then, that fiction so often explores the most inward, personal emotion of love?

It's not an easy task. Writers often struggle with finding the means by which to evoke emotions such as love or hate, with expressing sentiment in fiction without getting sentimental. And sex—well, good sex, at least—may be absolutely impossible to write about well, as Martin Amis says.

And yet writers are inevitably drawn to what Shirley Hazzard calls "a central element of existence."

Margot Livesey says that her novel *Banishing Verona* was partly about exploring the question: Can we ever know another person? In other words, can we really know our lover, or is he always a stranger? The question, of course, extends to parents, children, friends, and the other strangers that we love.

Perhaps what fiction attempts is just that: knowing another person.

Or, in the words of E. M. Forster: "Only connect."

## MARTIN AMIS

Sex is hard to write about because you lose the universal and succumb to the particular. We all have our different favorites. *Good* sex is impossible to write about. Lawrence and Updike have given it their all, and the result is still uneasy and unsure. It may be that good sex is something fiction just can't do— like dreams. Most of the sex in my novels is absolutely disastrous. Sex can be funny, but not very sexy.

## CHARLES BAXTER

The response to *The Feast of Love* has sometimes taken me by surprise. A week ago, a young couple came up to me in a bookstore and said that they had included a section of the novel in their marriage ceremony. I suppose that the book has struck a nerve in part because it treats romantic love as a kind of fever, a madness, and yet at the same time treats that fever quite seriously. In our era, the madness of romantic love can seem so old-fashioned or odd that novelists often simply don't want to deal with it. When readers don't like the book, it's usually because they feel that romantic love is passé or somehow needs more irony.

What I mean by "romantic love" was a form of obsessive

yearning that doesn't quite submit itself to reason. It's a close relative of infatuation. Occasionally readers would complain that in a book called *The Feast of Love* there were no mature adult relationships, but that wasn't the sort of book I wanted to write. The obsessional quality was the one I was doing my best to get at, dramatically, and so all the characters, young and old, necessarily had a lovelorn disposition—even Harry Ginsberg, who obsesses about his son.

## CLAIRE TRISTRAM

Desire in a general sense is a wish for something better, something that you don't have. My character desires to reconnect with a world that has been destroyed, and can only do that through sex. It's a more fundamental way of connecting with people, and it became my character's way of trying to reconnect with a world that has been destroyed around her.

## DOREEN BAINGANA

Sex is a metaphor for everything we humans are reaching for and trying out, failing and succeeding, including the fear of, the wish, and the way to connect with another human being. To get out of yourself and yet be really in yourself at the same moment is the mystery of sex and, in a wider sense, of being a conscious human being. Sex as a physical form of love becomes a concrete way to write about love, or the lack thereof. The writer must dwell on specifics, and one way to do this is to focus on action.

Sex represents desire for anything: money, stuff, a home, family, a partner, your worst or best and most intense self. This includes bad sex, sex for the "wrong" reasons, as well as good sex. Bad sex is more fun to write about than to do, of course, but it can also be more revelatory than good sex on the page. Also, the trajectory of your average sex act is the classic story line from rise to climax to fall.

Writing about sex for me is also about daring myself to go there. My family never, ever talked about it and hardly ever does so even now. I need to get out of safe and expected words, sentiments, and spaces in my writing, to escape the way we were taught to write at school, the way we were taught to think and use language. If I can write the unspeakable, then I can write about anything. It gives me the freedom to be bad, to be ungainly with language, to be unsophisticated, even crude, and more. Sometimes the result is good *new* writing.

I am fed up with the silences of my culture. Surely it is the writer's job to express what other people fear to say. For example, I have written about AIDS using sexual language, because we tend to avoid how lust is part and parcel of the disease, and instead use words like *prevention, abstinence, protection, medical studies, health care,* and other clean, euphemistic words.

Writing about sex is not as personally revealing as one might think, because like anything else you write about, the words are not the deed. I have not done those words, I have done and felt private things for which words such as *sex* and *lust* are only poor apologies.

## SHIRLEY HAZZARD

Love is perhaps the most interesting phenomenon. It's almost like a spell that's cast on us—falling in love, that is. There is nothing else like it in life, and I think it is a central element of existence—either the attaining of it or the lack of it, because the lack of love is a preoccupation of people. It's very obviously a part of our literary history; it has been a central concern to every writer, and that's because it's a central concern to everyone who lives.

Also, many things happen because of love; people withdraw from life or become violent for lack of love. And where there is not love, there is nothing.

## JOAN SILBER

It's not very hard to write about longing. Fiction has a lot of room for interior lyricism, and bits of the exterior world can be conjured up for the character's musings to attach themselves to. It's in dialogue that there's the greatest danger of being sentimental, but it strikes me that love is most convincingly shown in gesture or action rather than speech—in fiction as in life. And this especially applies to nonsexual love.

## PAM HOUSTON

In truth, for several years I said, with some authority, cowboys are no longer my weakness. Recently, they seem to have become my weakness again. The most recent cowboy takes the form of a poet. That's the thing about cowboys. They show up in the darnedest places. Their most lovable quality, I'm afraid, is their essential unavailability. We love them the way we love language. We want it to sit down and say what we want it to say. But it won't.

The dog in *Sight Hound* had a wider range of emotions than any man I dated in my twenties. In my universe, my dog talks to me. I would never consider myself a magical realist author. I spend half my day thinking about what my dog is thinking, and what he'd say if he could talk. In fiction, we often imagine dialogues for that character we either invented out of thin air or modeled after people we know. What I'm doing with my dog is really no different from that.

## HANNAH TINTI

There's a bunch of reasons why I write about animals in my short-story collection. One of them is I really like animals. But also I was interested in the animalistic side of human nature, and when and why humans or people cross over into doing very violent things. And another reason I think is that I was trying to use animals as a way of getting at readers' emotions. I think sometimes people open up their emotions to animals more easily than they do to other people. You see that with the way people get so obsessed with their pets. A big thing you see in New York is a person walking their dog with a diamond-stud collar, right past a homeless person. That interested me as well. The stories are about people, but I use animals as vehicles to get at the people.

## E. L. DOCTOROW

Theoretically, I should be able to get into anyone's mind. That's what the game is. Writing about people who are not you, and times before you lived, and places you've never seen.

## MARGOT LIVESEY

In *Banishing Verona,* I wanted to explore two questions that remain very pressing in my own life—namely, can we ever know another person, and can we ever know ourselves? And if the answer to both questions is no, then, how do we navigate our way through life?

The main character, Zeke, has Asperger's syndrome, and the difficulty he has in reading the world seems like a perfect metaphor for struggles that most of us have in understanding our interactions with each other. One thing I realized, interviewing people with Asperger's, was that many of them had difficulties understanding facial expressions. Talking to them made me realize how much we summarize when we say, "she smiled," or, "she frowned," and what a complex activity we go through when we utter those judgments, if you like, about other people. So one of the challenges of writing this novel was inhabiting a character who didn't take these shortcuts and who helped me and, I hope, my readers to look at the world from a fresh point of view.

I think I did get closer to an answer, but it's the kind of answer that is mostly about an ongoing experience rather than a finite or ultimate resolution. I think that, like my character Zeke, I'm someone who finds change, particularly changes in my own feelings, quite confounding. Writing the novel made me realize all over again that there's something hopeful about these changes as well as confusing.

## MICHAEL CUNNINGHAM

I write about a world in which everyone is queer, everyone is trying to live as best he or she can with repressions in society and in our own natures. To insist that these problems are particular to people of a certain sexual orientation seems a very small view of what *The Hours*, both the book and the movie, is trying to do.

## ANTHONY DOERR

I do feel that my books are about love: romantic love, the love characters have for each other, but also love for family, love for the landscapes in which they live, love for the miracle of being alive at a certain moment in a certain place. I don't at all think that science and nature sit at some opposite end of a spectrum from love. Fundamentally, a writer writes about his or her own love for people, for language, for a subject, for the world; I think the world is breathtaking and incredible and worth investigating, and I think most scientists feel that way, too. The more closely you look at something, the more miracles it reveals. Awe, mystery, love, fear—those are the fuels for both science and art.

I try to invoke wonder in my work, and I think wonder is all about being deeply, acutely in love: with the miracles and mysteries of the microscopic worlds, the human worlds, the astoundingly vast worlds of the cosmos. Ultimately, of course, we could say that all stories are about love. Love and death. And what is a story about death if it is not about love also? Death is about the cessation of love, the loss of familial love, a departure from the world that we have known and loved so briefly.

## GISH JEN

Are there any mothers that are not difficult? Now that I'm a mother myself, I understand not only what it is to have a difficult mother but also to be a difficult mother. I understand, too, that even the difficult mother is at some level blameless. My son has just turned thirteen, and when he went to the dentist, he was told that he's supposed to brush his teeth after breakfast, whereupon he turned to me and said in the most accusatory tone, "You told me to brush my teeth *before* breakfast! I've been doing it wrong all these years!" And all I could think was, This is a mother's fate.

I have to say that Mama Wong from *The Love Wife* is my very most favorite character. I am always greatly dismayed when someone says something like, "She's overbearing." Of course she is overbearing, but I don't want anyone to say anything mean about her, even if it's true. My mother, by the way, loved this book, including Mama Wong. She thought Mama Wong was great and, I must add, right.


ELIZABETH GRAVER

Parenting is a subject in all my novels. Both *The Honey Thief* and *Unravelling* have, at their hearts, children, though they move into adult life as well. As someone approaching my fortieth birthday, I wanted to write a book about an adult— about adult desire, adult ambivalence, about the huge, complicated project of trying to raise and nurture and care for children and also keep prior parts of one's self intact. When I began *Awake*, I was not yet pregnant with my first child. When I finished it, I had two little girls, the first now almost four, the second almost two. My novel is about the mother of two boys, ages nine and twelve, and I've not yet reached that stage, nor do I have boys, so I was still imagining that process. But the issues raised by parenting feel very urgent and central to me at the moment, since I am now a parent myself. How do you let your child explore the world, see it as an adventurous place full of wonder, and still keep her safe? How do you keep your own inner life going? How does a marriage or partnership change when children are added in? My little girls are teaching me a great deal; much of it, I imagine, will make its way into future works, in ways I can't imagine yet. Having kids has also taught me to slow down, look at the tiny details of life, in ways that have been very good for my writing. You watch a one-year-old examine a patch of grass for ten minutes and you start to see it differently too.

## ALISON SMITH

There's a great essay by Virginia Woolf called "On Being Ill," and she asks, why is illness not a great trope in literature . . . because love is a kind of illness, you feel feverish and consumed, and you're sort of separated from the world for a little while in either the passion of love or the passion of illness. I'm very taken with this point of view, and I hope someday to write a great novel about getting a cold.

In the meantime, I decided to write my experience, and I was blessed enough to fall in love when I was seventeen. The truth is I write about illness too, since I was anorexic, and the two are closely linked. The passion an adolescent girl feels, when it's sublimated—at the time I was taught to believe that falling in love with a woman was sinful—can turn into food issues. I think the eating disorder and the love affair were connected. When I was writing the book, there were two islands . . . and one was writing about my brother Roy dying, and that was excruciatingly hard, and the other island was the one with the nuns and the girls at my school. So when I was overwhelmed by the one, I would look at what else was in my life, and there was love and there was humor. I think I survived the loss of my brother because of the eccentric tutelage of the Sisters of Mercy, and because I had followed a forbidden passion. It's how I survived writing the book, too. Writing about a great kiss, and how I felt about that girl, was very pleasurable. In retrospect, you just remember: This person broke your heart. But if you slow down, you remember how great it was before the heartache, the hopes and the passions. It was sustaining to do that.

## MARISHA PESSL

I believe writers need to be chameleons, or like Meryl Streep, who can play all sorts of characters. A good writer should be able to cross gender lines and people of all social classes. So for me, writing from a male point of view would be a great challenge that I would look forward to taking on. I haven't done it, certainly not on the scale of a novel. Though in writing Gareth, he's a male point of view—making that particular character real, even though it's not first person.

## RICHARD FORD

What I know most about the subject of men and women is what the stories themselves contain. To try to provide an ex post facto gloss on those subjects is probably to imply that I know more than the story did, which, after writing the story, I'm sure is not true. I will say this about women and men: To me, women and men are much more interestingly alike or similar than they are dissimilar and un-alike. Relations between them, the sexual aspects notwithstanding, are to me just relations between two humans.

Insofar as I tend to think of characters not as human beings, I then don't really have to do much more than give a nod to gender per se. So what I'm doing is inventing lines of dialogue and inventing interior lives for putative women and putative men, so that the act of doing each is very similar.

## JOYCE CAROL OATES

I think that the concept of the so-called macho male writer is probably extinct, but these values are certainly prevailing in the culture. Most of my writer friends who are men are really feminists, though they may not write overtly about feminist subjects. They take for granted the equality of the sexes. Among my very masculine writer friends, who include Russell Banks, Richard Ford, and Robert Stone, I would say that their portraits of women are very convincing and very respectful.

## RICHARD BAUSCH

I have always considered myself lucky to be able to write about men and women with—I've been told, anyway—equal acuity and insight. Because I trust the subconscious, entirely. And having published a novel whose central characters are two women separated by a hundred years, I'm basically a weenie. How macho is that?

I hate all those designations. I want to do an anthology made up of stories about one-eyed homosexuals. Mailer published some great novels. Hemingway was a great writer. I hate all the designations. I've been called macho, and someone wanted me to be interviewed for a series called *The Rough South*. I turned them down. I don't like the designation.

How macho is Willa Cather? Yet she can make your blood jump. The murder scene in *O Pioneers!* Jesus. No male writer ever wrote a murder any better than that. So I bridle against the designations.

## THISBE NISSEN

For me, writing about love and sex is writing about the intimacies in which people seem to be the most vulnerable, and the most themselves—or at least the most revealing of themselves, whether that's consciously or not. I'm awed by a writer like Scott Spencer, who has spent his career navigating the excruciating intimacies between human beings. That's what I'm interested in, in life and in my work. I almost feel like I can't really help it; it's just what fascinates me.

# 9

# If at First You Don't Succeed . . .

## *Revise, Revise Again*

This is the work of writing.

Much rumination has gone on about the muse, from classical mythology to Shakespeare to *The Ghost Writer*—approaching inspiration as if it's a "Road to Damascus" miracle. Yet no poets pen romantic odes about third drafts. There's no Muse of Epic Revising. But I say: This is where the real miracle takes place.

Most anyone can have a great idea. A smaller group might get it onto paper in some form. A fair number of those will be able to revise parts of it until it is very, very good. Yet to take all the elements writers have talked about so far, to work out character and themes and place, to think about voice and style and language—it just doesn't happen in one fell swoop—to take what first comes out on the page and work it and work it and work it until every bit of it is right, until all of its parts become a beautiful whole: Only a very few writers will do that. True talent—perhaps even genius—lies not in coming up with the idea but in being able to do the hard, dogged work that brings that idea to fruition.

How do writers do it? This is one of the most difficult parts of writing to describe because, unlike character, which might start with a real person whom the reader has heard about, or place, which a reader might have visited, or theme, which can be bandied about in a seminar, revising is truly done at a desk, in a room, by oneself. It is the most solitary part of writing. Trusted readers or an editor may help, but even then, a writer must take their advice and go back and do it alone. What happens from head to hand to paper that changes this word to that? Therein lies the true mystery.

## MARIE ARANA

Revising is all.

I sometimes feel I'm flinging mud on the page. It's opaque, terribly formed, badly expressed. And then slowly, slowly, I begin to move it around. Thresh it. Squeeze it. And by the end of the day, I may have five hundred words of usable stuff.

To be a novelist, you have to let all the critical faculty go and be prepared to be the fool.

And then to edit yourself, you have to bring the ax back again, and be ruthless.

## TIM PARKS

I suppose I've become extremely elaborate in the way I work, otherwise it would be impossible to create the mixture of density with ease of flow. Every day I read at least twenty pages of whatever I'm working on to make sure I've got everything that's going on in my head. I do that on the computer. Then I'll get out the pencil and write three or four pages, which I transfer to computer at the end of the day.

Then the next day I'll work over and over them before starting the process all over again. Often I'm cutting as much as
adding. God knows if it's really necessary, but often all kinds
of exciting things happen. Since it slows the process down, it
keeps the mind open to possible plot developments you
might not otherwise have seen. Every month or so, I'll reread
the whole thing from scratch. But when I get to the end, suddenly, that's it. I've worked over it so much and so intensely,
it's finished. I hardly look at it again.

## MARTIN AMIS

I think you start with a situation, and it could be a derisory
situation, hardly anything happening, and then it accumu-
lates. The process of writing is really finding out more about
the novel. When you finish and then go back to revise, you're
amazed by your ignorance of what you were trying to do.
But it's really not divisible, I think, and you're bound to
reflect your time and your attitude to it and your culture,
willy-nilly. It's just part of the writing process.

## STUART DYBEK

The simplest answer I can give to a question as complex as
that is, at least so far as stories go, I've come to regard rewriting not first and foremost as an act of correcting mistakes, or
of editing, but rather as retelling the story. It is usually necessary for me to tell the story to myself numerous times before
it is a story ready to be told to a reader. In the process of
retelling the story, what needs to be corrected gets corrected,
what needs editing gets edited, but those are more often by-
products of the deeper process of retelling. There is an essen-

tial mystery at the heart of that process. If I read a story by a writer—let's say, Eudora Welty—my experience is that Eudora Welty has told me a story. If someone reads a story that I wrote, I presume they have the same take: Stuart Dybek told me a story. But who told Welty the story? Who tells the writer the story? True, sometimes we try to mimic experience or memory, and in those cases the challenge often seems having to measure up on the page to experience or memory and the allegiance that goes with it. But the longer I write, the more I think that it is illusory to think one is re-creating only from experience or only from memory—especially in fiction, which one chooses to write in order to have a primary allegiance to imagination. And once one departs from the factual events, even in the slightest, then there is that question: Who is telling you the story you are writing? Rewriting is the act—the state of consciousness—that is necessary in order to hear in clarity and completeness from that unnamed teller, until gradually and then finally the teller becomes oneself.

## ELIZABETH GRAVER

I revise just about every time I write; writing and revision are completely intertwined for me. Usually before I write on, I read over what I wrote the day before, sometimes starting all the way at the beginning. With each rereading, I make tiny changes, over and over again. Often this is good; I pare down or flesh out in ways that make the sentences, the characters, and the story stronger. Other times, I overwrite when I revise and have to go back (again) and distill, reduce, chop. That kind of sentence-by-sentence revising comes quite easily to me; I love language, to fiddle with words, to play with cadence and sentence structure. It's like layering paint, for me, or molding clay—very tactile, very satisfying. More challenging for me is the kind of global, architectural revision that comes toward the end of a draft, where sometimes you have to take away a whole section or radically rethink the way a book is built. For this kind of revision, I rely on readers—writer friends, my editor, etc.—who can help me see the project from a distance and take the long view.

## ART SPIEGELMAN

On September 11, after getting our son back from the United Nations School, a phone message from *The New Yorker* told Françoise Mouly, my wife, to head uptown to work on the *New Yorker* special issue four or five days hence. After realizing I was going to be no good at searching for bodies, I started searching for a cover idea, and I immediately starting barking up the wrong tree: an image that channeled Magritte, that a year later became the cover of a book called *A Hundred and Ten Stories*. It was a Magritte-like image, a picture of the two towers hovering in space covered by a shroud over the smaller buildings at Ground Zero, all against a beautiful blue sky. Françoise told me this wasn't going to fly—she's the covers editor—it was too beautiful, just like the day. I kept trying to make it work by dimming down the blue sky, but nothing worked until the screen was turned black. "There," I told Françoise, "it's going to have to be a black cover with a black tower," but I didn't quite mean it. And she immediately went off to get it made. I thought that since my first image had more to draw, it must be better. As a Jew, I've been brought up with the Protestant work ethic. Fortunately, cooler heads, Françoise's, prevailed.

## RICHARD BAUSCH

Once I thought I had a novel and it turned out it was only a short story. I wrote about eight hundred pages, but it ended up being a short story. And if it ever happens to me again, *I will go insane.* "All the Way in Flagstaff, Arizona." But it's not in the new book. I left it out. It's a story that makes me feel sick, because of what I had to go through. It's the first story I ever published, too, in *The Atlantic Monthly.*

How does an eight-hundred-page novel become a short story? Just like a kidney stone is passed.

## DAN CHAON

The real trick is to be able to forgive yourself for the bad writing you do or the forced writing you do, and to realize that first drafts are first drafts, and revision can turn forced writing into good stuff. To me, revision is so important a part of the process. So along with putting yourself on a schedule and writing every day, you have to let loose of the idea that if it's not flowing along perfectly, then it's not worthwhile to do. It's not as fun. But very often the stuff that comes through hard work and revision has more depth than the stuff that comes easily through inspiration.

## ANTHONY DOERR

For me, there are no clear divisions between revising and drafting. Those words used to scare me: I used to think, okay, a writer should write down a first draft of a story, start to finish, and then enter a new stage of production in which he revises it. But eventually I learned that I am always revising, eternally revising. There is probably a first draft inside my finished stories, engraved invisibly beneath all the revisions, but really the first draft is just a single sentence I've written down and immediately begun altering. Before adding a second sentence, I'm already revising the first one. Even after I have fifty pages, no paragraphs are safe; nothing feels completely revised. It's all exploration, all fumbling in the dark. Every morning, when I resume whatever it is I'm working on, I try to reread and revise as much as I can of what's already written, because in the morning I'm able to come to it with slightly new eyes; I can re-see it.

At the beginning, when you are conceiving a narrative and trying to understand where it might go, who its players might be, and what their needs are, you are already ruling out a near-infinity of possibilities because they don't feel right. It's instinctual. Toward the end, the process of revision works the same way; you come to it as a reader and try to understand what feels wrong.

Certainly, once a narrative is mostly formed and is, say, ninety percent delivered, then I'm often no longer able to identify exactly what is left to be done, and I leave it to my editor at Scribner, or, in the case of short stories, an editor of a magazine, to help me understand what more needs to be done.

MARISHA PESSL

Because I'd been working on *Special Topics in Calamity Physics* for three years and hadn't showed it to anyone—because I don't like to show drafts to people as I work, I'm incredibly private that way—I was anxious to finish and get it off, and I wrote a very sloppy final two chapters, which required rewriting after I found an agent.

With my editor, we worked primarily on excavating certain clues—bringing the clues of the mystery to light. Because I didn't have someone reading it, I thought the ending of the book would be incredibly obvious and certain twists wouldn't have an impact. So it was a question of bringing the clues out so the reader would see them as warnings or elements of suspense.

JOAN SILBER

One of the crucial changes my editor, Carol Houck Smith, asked me to make was in the beginning of the book *Ideas of Heaven: A Ring of Stories,* the first paragraph of the first story. She felt that it began in the wrong place. The story is called "My Shape," and it's narrated by a character who is talking about having a large bosom. Carol thought that if the book began like that, although it's a funny paragraph, it would misrepresent what the book was about. So we moved that paragraph and I wrote what I thought was a more suitable paragraph about longing, a longing for glamour and a longing for a more expansive life.

I just want to say that my experience with Carol has been particularly wonderful. She had a light hand, but she would edit at the level of the word, and we would have long discussions about certain words, which was quite fun.

CLAIRE TRISTRAM

I think writers really do love their editors. They're the first best reader you have. They buy the book because they love it.

My editor at Farrar, Straus and Giroux was John Glusman,
and in the first conversation I had with him, he explained my
book to me. It was just the most lovely feeling to have someone tell me what I had hoped I had written. Then he made
me work very hard. But all of the time I felt he was helping
me write the book I wanted to write, rather than what he
would want me to write. I think he's an uncommon editor,
but I think editors go into the business because they love
finding a book they want to acquire, so I think that's something every writer can look forward to when they get
published.

## ALISON SMITH

I think I learned how to revise by writing *Name All the
Animals*. I had this eight-hundred-page monster, and I had
absolutely no idea what to do. I had experience revising
twenty-five-page stories, but not a book. I had to learn to go
small. I had to learn to say, you don't know what to do with
eight hundred pages, but what about this sentence. I would
sometimes start with, do you want this comma? Now, let's
look at the sentence. Now, let's look at the paragraph. I don't
do that exactly now, but I'm still breaking things down into
bite-size pieces. I have a document that's as long as or longer
than any document I work on, and that's the process document. Writing about a chapter, a treatment for a chapter, what
has to happen to these characters in this chapter.

For *Name All the Animals*, there were so many craft elements to face, I would reread my favorite writers and I'd say,
This time when you read this book, look at how Charlotte
Brontë structured a chapter. And this time when you read this
book, let's look at dialogue and which parts are spoken and

which parts are told indirectly. And it was really exciting. It was like going behind the scenes of your favorite book and seeing them again.

## TOD GOLDBERG

Writing a great deal and becoming somewhat dispassionate about your own work helps. Very few people can look at their own work and say, "Oh, this is crap, this is great, this is more crap," but at some point along the way I, at least, was able to pick up where I was just phoning it in. Being able to correct it, not so much. But novel writing has given me an insight that short stories never had: novels are enormous living creatures. There is so much white space to fill in, so much time involved, that you are forced to become a different reader and writer in the process.

I don't think the best writers are the best readers, but I think they are different readers. I guess I'm often caught looking for the Wizard behind the curtain when reading my favorite books, and in some ways that stops it from being just a good temporal experience.

## PAM HOUSTON

Close reading is a skill that develops over time, surely. But I think kids who grow up in difficult or dangerous households are particularly close readers. They know how to pick up on the most subtle cues—it's a survival skill. I credit my skill as a trained observer, which makes me both a better writer and a better reader of my students' work, to my difficult childhood. I will say that finishing a novel gave me a greater understanding of my students who were writing novels, but the ability to read closely for the story under the story—that training goes way back.

The best writers aren't always the best readers. I know that from classes. I mean, I think the same skill that makes me able to notice the precise detail in the world that I'm going to bring back to the page in my own story is the skill that lets me see underneath the students' language to the story they're trying to write.

## JOYCE CAROL OATES

The first draft is definitely the hardest, like hacking one's way through a thick jungle with something like a butter knife. By far the most pleasurable aspect is the final revision, which is like soaring over the jungle in an airplane that you are piloting.

## RICHARD FORD

When I wrote the story "Communist," which was in 1983 in Mississippi—far from Montana, where the story is set—I wrote the story to an end that didn't feel like the right end although it felt like an end. I showed the story to my friend Joyce Carol Oates, and she gave me the best advice any other writer has ever given me. She said, "Richard, you need to write more on this story. Write more words." And I had to figure out what more words to write.

# Are We There Yet?

## *Knowing When a Novel or Story Is Finished*

And they all lived happily ever after.

That's not the way much contemporary fiction ends—and if it did, most readers would suspect that the author was being ironic.

And yet, even in this day where the once-shocking postmodern tendencies of Borges and Barthelme have become almost commonplace, authors do desire to bring their work to a conclusion. Not to tie up loose ends into a pretty bow. But to write, well, an ending.

I think of Donald Barthelme's famous story "Views of My Father Weeping." On the last page, the narrator finds out what happened when his father was killed—maybe. The "truth" of what he has found out is immediately questioned. The story ends with "Etc."

A reader might, at first, think that Barthelme was cheating and not giving us an ending at all. Etc.? But that is exactly the point. No one ever resolves the complicated, contradictory feelings one has about a difficult father, or any father, mother, sister, lover. The uncertainties and conflicts will go on and on and on. Etc.? Absolutely.

Such a rounding-out of themes, without false conclusions, is what most writers here talk about wanting in an ending. A feeling of being full, Richard Ford calls it. A sense, John Dalton says, that "the emotional journey is complete."

## JOYCE CAROL OATES

Depending upon the genre you're writing in, there are different ways of establishing what we call closure. For instance, if you're writing a very short piece, such as a poem or a prose poem, or a "miniature narrative," you can actually print out variants of the work and have two or three or more endings. And you can read through them quickly and live with them for a few days or weeks and see, in a kind of dispassionate way, what seems best.

If you have a longer work, such as a novel, obviously you can't do quite the same thing. But you can have alternative endings. My own way of writing is very meditated and, despite my reputation, rather slow-moving. So I do spend a good deal of time contemplating endings. The final ending is usually arrived at simply by intuition. (Sometimes an editor will have a comment. An editor may feel an ending is too abrupt, since I try to have dramatic endings, so I would revisit that work and see if what the editor has said might be valid.)

## RICHARD BAUSCH

I don't really choose those moments; they choose me. That moment comes up, and then I know the story's done. It's almost as if I'm listening to a symphony, and you just know that it's coming to an end. That happens in the prose for me, where there's a cadence that takes over in the prose, it's hitting its notes here, it's coming to the end. And I don't always know what the story means, particularly.

In "Valor" [in which a man saves people from a bus accident, then his wife still leaves him], I had no idea that any of that was going to happen. I had no idea that when he was ready to lie about why he was in the bar, that he would find he has to tell the truth, because he's done this brave thing, and he would feel he'd dishonor it if he lied. Though the story doesn't say that.

It took me a long time to learn that the most valorous thing he does in that story is touch his wife's shoulder, so she knows she doesn't have anything to fear from him.

## STUART DYBEK

I've never been able to answer that question. For me it's just a gut level. Sometimes it comes in a flash. Sometimes it's got to lie around for a while. If somebody else believes it's done, then you start believing it's done.

A book becomes a design, and maybe at a gut level you feel you've completed the design, the book is over. But it doesn't necessarily mean the stories don't stop coming.

## MARIE ARANA

Sometimes you slop over and write a lot more than you have to.

I did.

I wrote a huge afterword, Victorian style, in which all my

characters went off and had lives beyond the story. It was fun to imagine.

But when I put on my editorial hat and looked at it in the cold light of day, I saw that I had to lop it off a lot sooner.

Some writers—John Irving, for instance—write the end first. I'm not kidding. He told me he does this. He cannot begin a book until he has the last sentence!

That I can *not* imagine.


## JOANNA SCOTT

There are two points of exhilaration for me when I'm writing. There's the point when I think, I've got something here and can keep going. And then there's the point when I write the final word, and I say, "Okay, that's done."

I once heard William Gaddis say he wrote long books because he didn't like them to end. And I can understand that. The satisfaction of writing a book lasts longer than the satisfaction of finishing a book.


## ANTHONY DOERR

I feel like if you don't know the ending before you start—this isn't true for all writers, and it's also encouraging to my students when they hear some of their favorite writers didn't know the ending of their books—it's easier to surprise yourself and be inventive if you allow yourself the room to do so, if you don't try to execute an outline. But then of course you reach a point where you have to say, "I've got to figure out how this book's going to end." Otherwise, you're going to write yourself into so many dead ends.

With *About Grace*, I knew what would happen to Grace

early on, but I was probably two-thirds of the way through
the book before I knew how to execute the ending. I didn't
know until I was closer to it.


## ALISON SMITH

The ending of *Name All the Animals* changed like forty-seven
times. I wrote the book for six years while working as a wait-
ress and having three housemates in this little town. And
everyone was wondering if I was working on a book or qui-
etly going mad. Everyone does go a little mad as a writer. A
lot of people said, "You must be done by now," and there was
a bit of a danger of going Casaubon, the man Dorothea married in *Middlemarch*. But I was sort of offended when people
would say, "The book probably needs to be taken away from
you, you're probably done." I'd say, "No, I'm going to know
when it's done." And the truth is I did.

The final year was a real watershed. It took that long to
travel the distance between my brother's dying and first love.
When I started to get that structure right, within six months
I cut forty thousand words and I wrote forty thousand words.
It was the most exciting year of my writing life, and it was
just me at my computer, when I started to get it. That's why
now when I have really bad days at my computer, I see it as
just putting in the hours, waiting. You really have to put in the
hours in order to get to that epiphany.


## HANNAH TINTI

I often describe my way of writing as using a divining rod. I
mentally picture the fork-shaped branch and just try to let go
and let it guide me. I think the story is off in one direction

and then it will suddenly veer left and hit a spot I wouldn't have expected. My endings come this way as well, driven by the emotion of the piece, and often sooner than I planned for. The hard part is going back and making the changes to the text so that it all bends properly in the right way— inserting road signs, basically—so that when the end appears, the readers feel that they've arrived at the right place.

## JOHN McNALLY

*The Book of Ralph* kept growing as I went along—you start finding yourself creating things you wouldn't have created by virtue of the way you're putting it together. I wanted short-shorts in between, and have them focus on place, but I didn't have a plan going into it. When I thought the book was done, I thought there was a missing piece, when these two charac-ters first met. It's the last thing I wrote for the book—which then worked well for me, in terms of the last story. When they first meet, it's a story in which the kids in fifth grade put together a diorama of the future. Ralph, who's failed two grades, puts together a diorama, and the city hasn't changed at all. The final chapter then is the future, and we see that the city hasn't changed any. Originally I had it sequential, then it made sense to juxtapose the last chapter.

## CHARLES BAXTER

As Evan Connell is reputed to have said, "I'm done when I start to put back the commas that I've just taken out." In my own case, I'm finished with a book when I can't think of a single thing more to do to it, or for it, or with it. Sometimes amateur readers or editors will help me out with suggestions—point out the gaps or the excesses—but otherwise I quit when I'm blind to further improvements. (If I still see something wrong with a book, I won't let it out of my sight until I've devised a solution.)

## JOAN SILBER

Endings are usually hard for me, though occasionally something just comes as a gift. There's a danger of relying too much on an image—that's a modern kind of corniness. Usually the story has ended dramatically before I've come to the end, but I want the final paragraph to point to what's thematically important—to what I want the reader to make of all this. Since I often have long, rambling plots, this is my moment to suggest I know what I'm doing.

## THISBE NISSEN

Perfect? Never. Exhausted? Yes. I think there comes a point when I've learned all I can learn from a piece, or when continued futzing isn't going to make it better; it's going to make it gummy, like when you stir the stuffing too much before you put it in the turkey. Or, to continue the Thanksgiving metaphor, I vastly prefer a lumpy, homemade gravy to one smoothed and stabilized with additives that emerges from the microwave in all its processed glory. Or, to trot out another metaphor entirely: I can't stand how Broadway musicals these days are all miked and amped and computerized. I like to see the spit fly from the actors' mouths! I like to see the sweat! Maybe I'm just more interested in writers and process than I am in the finished product. The humanity of it is in the flaws. I'm finished when I can't make it any better, which doesn't mean it couldn't *be* better, but it's the best *I* can make it, as the writer I am, the person I am. Then it's time to move on and use what I've learned for the next project. I'm not aiming for perfecting; I'm aiming to keep writing and learning. My goal isn't to write the perfect book; it's to live a sustainable life, writing sustainably.

## JOHN DALTON

The ending for *Heaven Lake*—that is, the actual words that comprise the ending—came to me while I was working out on my ancient NordicTrack. But the events that end the novel came into focus gradually. To realize these events—and to recognize that they were the right events—I first had to be certain what the novel was about thematically.

With an ending, I want to invent a concluding incident that in some graceful way comments on the important themes I've set up throughout the novel. And I want to wrap up some, but not all, of the plot lines so that the novel feels like life—some issues resolved, others open-ended.

Finishing a novel is an intensely emotional experience, and it's easy to get a bit drunk on those rich emotions and wind up writing something that's sentimental or a bit melodramatic. So it's a fight to the very end to keep things compelling but *understated*.

I think you have to have an instinctual sense that the arc of the book and the pacing will satisfy the reader, and that, by the final page, the emotional journey is complete. As for the question of whether the writing has reached a level where it can be considered finished, I'd suggest printing out all the pages and making a proud stack of them on your dinner table. Then start flipping open the manuscript randomly.

Begin reading wherever your gaze falls on the page. If you keep doing this and what you read continues to strike you as compelling and elegantly composed, this may be a sign that you're finished.

## MARISHA PESSL

There's an old movie of Alfred Hitchcock's from 1944 called *Lifeboat*. Several survivors of a torpedoed ship find themselves in the same boat. And I think writing a book is like this. You're stuck in a rowboat in the middle of the ocean, and your characters are the people you're going to have to make it to safety with—so they'd better be strong. They'd better be fascinating and entertaining, because you don't know how long you're going to be floating out there with them—with no land in sight.

You're finished with a novel when, at last, you've come upon relatively dry land and you just can't row anymore.

## FRANCES ITANI

When I am writing a story or a novel, the ending almost always comes to me about three-quarters of the way through. This usually happens while I am out walking—I try to walk a couple of miles every day, and this helps me to solve problems in my work. My theory about endings is that the ending must not be forced. It will become absolutely inevitable and must evolve from the work itself. I'll go even further and say that it's quite possible for the reader to reach the "expectation of ending" at the same point at which it occurred to the writer. The "twinning of the minds" here, between creator and reader, and the inevitability factor, can be quite wonderful.

## TOD GOLDBERG

Endings have never been my strong suit, both in writing and in my interpersonal relationships, but at least with writing I can recognize the signs more clearly. Not to sound too mystical, but as I work toward the end of a novel or a short story, the characters won't let me rest—they keep up an incessant chatter in my mind that is a bit like a Ouija board gone haywire: Yes, this is how my life should go; No, this is not where I should end up. And so everything starts to become clear, about how these fictional lives will go on after the last page is written. In order for me to provide that opportunity for the characters, I have to give them an ending that isn't an ending at all. There's no white space in real life, there are no space breaks or dramatic pauses, so I know my story is done when I can fully appreciate the consequences of all my characters' actions, can foresee how the rest of their lives might shake out. And if I can see it, then the reader can see it, and that sense of spontaneity will be lost in short order. That's when I know that I've found the end.

## RICHARD FORD

I think a novel is finished when I go through it and I don't want to change anything. Novels achieve different effects with different sorts of ending gestures. Maybe the sense of how an ending feels is quite visceral to me. I plan for where I want a book to end spatially, but, as with *Independence Day*, I got to the end of that plan and then it wasn't right. So I had to knock that end off, much to my publisher's chagrin, and write a new one. In a very traditional way, I want an end to be dramatic in a localized sense, and I want it to be in some

ways conclusive of the major concerns of the book that I just
wrote. Knowing whether or not I've done that is also very
intuitive. There is a sense to an ending in my practice that
feels very full. I feel like all of the things that have been in the
book up to now have sort of, in a sense, been fully
terminated.


## MARY KAY ZURAVLEFF

I'm writing to match some tune in my head, some flavor
from a dream, translated into words on a page. The first few
drafts, my people move monstrously through contrived
mazes. Eventually, I can stop pounding on their chests and
filling their lungs. They'll sit up and blink, and then, to my
amazement, samba down a path far more imaginative and
inevitable than what I'd envisioned.

Once we're all satisfied, there are still drafts devoted to language and description, gestures and observations. When I
make a pass for smells, I'm almost done. For both of my novels, I gave a draft to a few choice critics whose exceptional
advice was on the order of, "I almost see the constellation
you were aiming at, but you missed a star here. And here."
Then I rewrite it one more time.

# 11

# The Writing Life

## *Springs of Hope, Winters of Despair*

In the morning, she takes long walks to clear her head, then does a little research for her novel. In the afternoon, she makes lunch while reading the latest *New Yorker*, then meets a writing friend for coffee. She has an idea and writes it down in her notebook. At night, she dresses in black and heads off to her editor's for a book party. The next week, she wins the Pulitzer.

How many clichés of the writing life exist in the world? The hip young author in New York. The writer who moves to a cottage in the woods, inspiration swooping down like a bird. Hemingway-esque hard-drinking bullfighters, party-goers like Capote. Clichés, every single one. And, like most clichés, the biggest problem with them is that they are completely inaccurate: No one's ever doing any writing.

The writing life, mostly, is work. If you work hard enough, keep sending stuff out, you may feel the exhilaration of being published for the first time. Then, every few years or so, if you're lucky, there's publication and the distracting world that surrounds it—reviews, readings, interviews, signings. But that's not writing. Most days are a struggle between writing and staving off all the other things you should be doing. Few writers make enough money to allow them to do nothing but write. So they teach, or temp, or wait tables, or work at Morgan Stanley. This is the writing life? It's like making a doctor write a best-selling mystery novel so he could afford to see patients three days a week.

There are moments of glory. They rarely come at prize ceremonies or at a party with famous writers. They come on the battleground—at your desk, writing. A good sentence. An idea that shapes your novel.

Writers do it because they want to, they do it because they have to, they do it because they don't really know what else they possibly could do. "I'm cursed!" Joanna Scott says. But I don't think she minds. Writing is a passion. Which is perhaps where all those romantic notions come sweeping in.


## JOYCE CAROL OATES

I have lots of wonderful days. I have many wonderful days that are too quiet and unsensational even to take note of. A very nice day would have work in the morning and some accomplishment, however small; an afternoon with my husband on some outing like jogging or bicycling on country roads here in rural New Jersey; a return in the late afternoon to work again; and maybe an evening with friends in Princeton.


## RICHARD FORD

I just bought a new notebook at the bookstore, and I made my first entry in it on the plane the other day. It is a daybook, a kind of grab bag, without order, without rules, that I don't feel the least bit indebted to, unless there's something I want to put in it. It's kind of a substitute for a memory, something I used to have, and it also is a reminder of what I'm on the earth to do. Notice and make things out of it.

## MICHAEL CUNNINGHAM

Some days I find it a pleasurable experience. Some days I'd rather do just about anything else. Every writer seems to need to develop his or her own relationship to the process. I know writers who write sporadically, in huge fits of inspiration, and then nothing for long periods. I know writers who write in pure agony one hour a day, which is all they can bear.

I did reach the point of despair, more than once, as the years went by, and I just couldn't give any of this stuff away. And I reached a point at which I decided, I'm just going to keep writing even if no one ever publishes anything. And what happened is I stopped trying to write what I thought someone would publish, and that's when people started publishing me. It was only when I stopped trying to please and started to write what mattered most to me that it all took off.

## COLM TÓIBÍN

I think most of life, including Henry James's life, is adrift. And you don't ever have to make a choice. He tended to get great satisfaction from work, and he worked very hard. I have a feeling that work made him happy. And the problem arises then, if he hadn't worked, he would have been unhappy, and by working so hard, he missed out on other things. And that, too, left him unhappy. There is no equilibrium. I think those decisions never get made. But I think an artist can have both, and a great number of artists end up being quite happy in their personal lives. Don't ask me to name them! But there certainly are. It isn't part of the deal that you have to be personally unhappy.


## MARTIN AMIS

Sometimes there's a kind of crazy-scientist cackle that comes from my study. But it's a mixture of anxiety as well as comic energy that you feel sometimes flowing through you, and you always have to balance it with self-doubt and self-reproach.

I don't think any interesting work of art can possibly be depressing—otherwise, *King Lear* would kill more people than cholera. If it's good, it's cathartic, and the reader feels purged and renewed. I think the reader who gets depressed by *The Information* is probably depressed to begin with, although I would say that that novel was written under heavy skies. *Yellow Dog* felt more high-pressure—the sky above was clear.


## ALICE McDERMOTT

I have learned that the most disruptive thing you can do to your writing life is publish something. . . . Amid all the other demands of normal living, you carve out some time to sit around and make up stories, and then you publish a book and suddenly you're supposed to travel all over and meet people and give interviews and visit book clubs—all of which you do, of course, because you're grateful to your readers, and to your publisher, and to anyone at all who feels kindly toward literary fiction . . . but the time and silence and shedding of self-consciousness so necessary to the writing of fiction slowly seeps away. Fortunately, literary novels (and the people who write them) have a short shelf life in the public arena, and eventually you get to return to the work . . . and on the days it doesn't go well, you find yourself thinking, Why doesn't someone call and disrupt me?

I'm sure everything that happens to us while we're living life (rather than writing about it) informs our fiction in some way, but I would be hard-pressed to know precisely how motherhood has changed or altered my fiction. I know how it changes my writing life. (My ten-year-old, for instance, came home from school this morning with a cold and is, at the moment, trying to tell me something he just read in *Lord of the Rings*, even as I write this.) No doubt motherhood has something to do with all the notes in my journal that tend to trail off . . . but in some way I guess I believe the novels themselves exist in a world that has little to do with my own daily life. . . .

## MARY KAY ZURAVLEFF

This morning, my four-year-old was wearing shorts and a T-shirt with a cowgirl outfit over it, which slid down her hips as we tried to cross Connecticut Avenue. I have a great excuse for the fact that her hair wasn't brushed—her mother's a writer.

Annie Dillard says it takes five to ten years to write a novel. Some people do it in a year, but some people can lift cars. I did have a struggle with this book, *The Bowl Is Already Broken*, which is more complicated and ambitious than my first. One strange complication was, three years into writing about a woman who was pregnant and didn't know it, I was pregnant and didn't know it! My editor says I'm the only woman who's ever gotten pregnant from writing.

So life intervened in all its complicated ways. Then I kept rewriting the first part of the book, which turned out to be something of a burden, because I didn't actually know where the book was going until I'd finally finished a complete draft. There were chunks of time when I couldn't write, and then I'd have to relearn the book. Meanwhile, I was growing into the age of the main character. When I started, I was thirty-five and Promise was forty-three. When I finished, she was still forty-three and I was forty-four, and I'd learned a few things along the way.

### JOHN MCNALLY

There have been times it's more difficult than other times, and I've had to work three jobs, adjunct teach, sign up for Manpower and do data entry, and try to sneak in writing when I could, sometimes on the job. Those were always the jobs that I looked for, working in a library. I'd wait for everybody to leave for lunch and pull out my stuff and start working.

But now I have a good teaching load so I can have a daily schedule. Travel disrupts it horribly. The older I get, the more I'm set in my ways. I used to be able to write anywhere, and now, if a dog barks three blocks away, it drives me crazy.

### ANTHONY DOERR

It took me about three years to write *About Grace*. I wasn't teaching for two of those years, so I was working eight-hour days, five days a week. And it would include research and reading—it wasn't just a blank page, laying down words. I found my first novel difficult. I don't want to make it sound like it's any more difficult than driving a cab or going to any other job, but there are so many opportunities for self-doubt that you just kind of need to soldier on. I had a big sign on my desk saying, No Failures of Nerve. It's so easy to get up and go downstairs and check your e-mail. I just wanted to train myself to sit there and just think through the problem. It's really similar to working out. You just have to force yourself to do it, and it feels good when you do it. I've run a few marathons—the same thing as writing a novel, although not quite.

## ALISON SMITH

Before I began working on *Name All the Animals,* I went on a scholarship to the Bennington Summer Writing Workshops. It's a summer writing institute, and my teacher was Rick Moody. I was working then on what I thought was going to be my first book. It was a novel that was a reinterpretation of four Greek myths. It was a very technical intellectual exercise. It was all in the head. But I was pretty excited about it, and I showed about forty pages of it to Rick Moody, and he said, "You know, this is technically proficient—you know what you're doing. The writing is good. But I don't care. Do you care?" And he said, "You're going to be with this material for a long time. Are you going to be able to be passionate about this?"

No one had ever really responded with this kind of emotional, big-picture response, and I was fascinated and offended. But he's a very disarming person and he said, "What if you wrote a completely autobiographical, completely sentimental story?" I was totally confused. And I said, "But nothing ever happened to me really." But I did it that weekend and showed it to him the next week. The story was just a little exercise—I wrote about going to summer camp when I was twelve. Nothing newsworthy happened to me at summer camp. I hated it. So it was about the experience of going to summer camp, a coming of age. I showed it to him and he said, "Now this is interesting." And I was really confused. I could not see how my life could be more interesting than a Greek myth.

After that experience, I had a bit of a crisis with my work. I went home and for the first time in a long time I stopped writing. I reread my journals, which I had been keeping since I was fourteen, and I looked at what I was writing when I was not trying to create great literature. I realized that what I'd been writing about for more than ten years was my family, and my brother, and what it was like to grow up with him and what it was like to lose him. So it was about six months into that self-examination that I started to write again, and I said, "I'm going to write a story about my family."

## CLAIRE TRISTRAM

When I was writing what became my first novel, *After*, I was prepared not to be published because of what I wanted to write. I didn't want to write a happy-ending book, and that would be easier getting published.

So for me it was a happy feeling. A great publisher picked it up and I got a chance to be heard that way. I was at my mother-in-law's and she took a picture of me when I got off the phone with my agent, and I look very happy. It's very close to how I looked on my wedding day.

## JOHN DALTON

When you spend eight years writing a novel, you're taking a real gamble with your life. You're not doing what all your friends are doing, establishing themselves in a career, having kids. I feel like I survived the gamble by the skin of my teeth.

I was happy, but it was much more rewarding to me as I went through the publishing process. Moments like holding the book in your hands were more powerful than when I found out it was sold. I never really believe that anybody would read the book aside from my family, and I'm still finding it strange that someone I don't know and have no connection to is reading the book. And it's very pleasing, it's very satisfying.

## HANNAH TINTI

The very first time I was published was in a magazine. It sounds very strange, but since that was the first time, everything pales in comparison. I came home from work and on my machine was a message from Lois Rosenthal, who was editor of *Story* magazine. I still have the little answering-machine tape with her message on it. It is a validation of a gamble that you take with your life. I had worked so hard and for so long. And you make a lot of personal sacrifices in your life in order to be a writer. And so it was thrilling to think I was right in making this choice.

## CHARLES BAXTER

Well, it's better to be nominated for awards than not to be nominated for them, but of course to some degree such

awards are always subjective. And yet they point to an enthusiasm that the judges have had and can defend. The second
part is the important one: I have certain indefensible enthu-
siasms, but the ones I *can* defend are the ones to pay attention
to. When you can be articulate about some book you've
liked, your enthusiasm really counts. As long as you have rea-
sonably fair-minded judges (and the National Book Awards
panel almost always has had them), I'm relatively comfortable
with it. The year I was nominated, I lost to Susan Sontag, and
I didn't mind at all. Really. But literature is not a sack race.
There aren't real winners and losers in the Republic of
Letters, not in that way.

ELIZABETH GRAVER

When my first book came out, in 1991, Richard Ford told
me, in response to my anxiety about the pressures of publishing, reviews, reactions, sales: "You need to make an island
apart from all that, where you do the work." Writing, at its
essence, makes me happy. It allows me to explore things,
move inside them, however dark the subjects themselves. It
has become a way I live in the world, a way of trying to ask
questions, make meaning, live inside language. I need to do
it, and I think I would be doing it whether I was getting
published or not. This said, there are these practical consid-
erations. I am lucky to have a very good teaching job and a
very supportive editor and literary agent. I earn a living by
both teaching and writing, and that helps balance things out
a bit and makes my situation feel more secure. The thing that
feels in short supply for me right now—as the mother of
two small children, a writer, and a professor—is time. I am
always trying to find more time to write without compro-

mising other pieces of my life. When I do find that time, I usually manage to let the real world drop away and inhabit the imaginary world I am creating. I don't fret, then, about whether the book will sell or not; I think I would, for one, be incapable of predicting, and I am also too deep inside a kind of dream world for such questions to feel relevant. Later, when the book comes out, I might fuss about it more, but by then it's out of my hands. On a more positive note, I think the rise of reading groups has been a great thing. There are a lot of thoughtful people out there who are reading literary fiction and looking for stories that are not quick fixes or page-turners.

## JOANNA SCOTT

Something I have been asking myself in recent years has been, "Is this getting easier, or not?" I think mostly not, is the answer to that question. If anything, it's getting harder.

I've been spending my days recently wandering through Florence, gazing at great art and thinking about the muscular expressive art of a great artist like Michelangelo and the quieter, restrained art of a great artist like del Sarto. He was called the artist *senza errore*, the artist who makes no mistakes. And I have found myself wanting to strive for that kind of gentle perfection, the restraint, the polish, a more tranquil beauty. Perhaps less expressive beauty, but still provocative and mysterious.

So, I hope the general aesthetic challenges I set myself will get harder. I want them to be harder. The blank space between the end of one book and the beginning of the next is just as blank as ever. But I think I've learned some things over the years.

## THISBE NISSEN

I am not a very disciplined writer, I'm somewhat embarrassed to say. But I guess my feeling is that somewhere along the way, I seem to get things done. As long as that keeps working without having to implement a schedule for myself, I'm just going with it. It's possible that I write in some sort of fugue state that I then forget. I have very little memory of sitting down to write—it all just happens along the way. I'm not someone to use as an example in terms of discipline.

I feel like part of the reason that I love writing is that I'll always feel young when I start something or when I'm in the middle of something or when I finish something. There was a point—I recall it very specifically—the point in college when I had been writing pretty seriously and I had this understanding that this was something I would never figure out completely and thus would always be a challenge and a puzzle. And that really is the way I still feel about it. I can't imagine that's going to change anytime soon.

## A. S. BYATT

I spend a lot of my time watching tennis. Tennis players are old when they're Agassi's age, whereas writers, particularly writers who write long novels, they are only starting at Agassi's age.

I knew that as a little girl. I knew I had chosen a profession for old people. I hated being a novelist when I was twenty— I had nothing to write about. So my life now is a kind of small window of having the knowledge and not dying.

I think aging is a very interesting process. I've been watching the television in this hotel room this morning, and it's full of denial of aging. There's a huge program on how you can have your whole body remade so you can look thirty. Nevertheless, aging does and will take place, and is in fact very frightening, because many of us are living into terrible incapacity. We get Alzheimer's, but we don't die.

That's the first part of the answer. The second part is this isn't what I'm experiencing myself.

I like the kind of independence of this brief period of my life when you don't feel physically "really" old, and I know that my work is better than it ever has been. So I feel kind of gleeful. But I also know it won't last very long. So I think I should look at aging while I'm still physically fit enough to look at it objectively. So far it's been fun, but any moment now it will cease to be fun.

# 12

## Musing About the Muse

### *How Writers Find Inspiration*
### *When It Doesn't Find Them*

Writers find inspiration at their desks. This is the hard truth that many people don't wish to believe.

Not in a plane, not in a train, as Sam I Am might say. Not in a car, not in a bar.

Which is not to say that writers don't get ideas in strange, fascinating places, and that they don't see those ideas come to life in mysterious ways. Edward P. Jones had *The Known World* knocking around in his head for a decade before he sat down and wrote it in two and a half months. Margot Livesey calls *Eva Moves the Furniture* "a love song" to her dead mother and says she felt almost in contact with her as the last chapter flowed out in nearly one sitting. One might suspect the presence of a muse in these stories.

John Dalton heard a drunk man ask a group of American teachers in Taiwan if anyone wanted to marry the love of his life so she could get out of China, get divorced, and marry him. Dalton thought: Here is a novel.

But writing *Heaven Lake* took Dalton *eight years*. Inspiration is more than just an idea—more than a few hours, even a few days, of feeling inspired. One must then go about implementing that idea. It's a daily practice. Think of all the ideas that one novel, even one short story, encompasses. Each word in that last sentence was an idea. Writing the word *novel,* thinking of writing "one short story or novel," then switching the order . . . every one of those thoughts is an idea. And this little intro isn't exactly *Paradise Lost.*

Not in a house, not with a mouse, not in a plane, not on a train.

Looking for inspiration? The muse is at your desk. Go say hello.

## TOBIAS WOLFF

I cannot wait for inspiration to grab me by the throat. Life is too busy for that. If it grabs me by the throat when I'm having my car washed, what am I supposed to do? I have to go to my desk like everybody else and hope that I will be given what I need to continue writing each day when I'm there. But I have to be at my desk in order to receive the gift.

## MICHAEL CUNNINGHAM

What I do is this: I get up every morning and go straight to work, and on the good days I write with pleasure. On the bad days, I just sit there, waiting to see if something will come. On the bad days, if I'm lucky, I'll come up with a lame sentence or two, thinking, I'll delete this later. It's terrible, but it's all I've got today. I've found, though, that when I look back six months later at what I've written, I can't distinguish the parts I wrote on the good days from the parts I wrote on the bad. I've come to believe that the inspiration is always there, like an electrical current, and what varies is our access to it. And I've found that the best way to cope with that is with diligence, with a kind of daily determination.


## TOD GOLDBERG

My students always ask me where my stories come from, as if there's some secret well filled with fiction and all they need are directions to plug into MapQuest, and I always tell them the same thing: That great stories come from the same place as bad stories but that it's our job as writers to show the peculiarity of human life in such a way that it's hard to tell the difference.


## CHARLES BAXTER

It's interesting: I don't have any idea of what my next book will be. I feel a bit wrung out, like a washrag. I'll have to daydream my way into my next project, whatever it will be. So far, no new book has appeared on my imagination's horizon.


## MARIE ARANA

Sitting down every day, waiting for the words to come, being disciplined about the time: That's the real work. And eventually, the gears start in.

I'm always surprised at how characters can run in and just carry that ball for you.

Writing nonfiction is like carving a rock. It sits there. It's hard. It's big. And you whittle away at something concrete.

Writing fiction is like pulling things out of the air. Nothing is there but invention. It's disconcerting, thrilling.

Some of us in the fire of writing fiction end up running around and doing a lot of research just to weigh the process down a little and make it more real.

I'd love to get back to nonfiction some day (and I have idle dreams about writing a major biography—don't have a clue whose), but fiction keeps pulling me away. I hear a phrase, or someone says something about a wayward aunt, and my mind goes off constructing worlds. If only there were time enough to do it all.

## STUART DYBEK

Ray Carver, who was a friend, used to say he couldn't write fiction without writing poetry, and that's very true for me, if only because I loot the poems for fiction. I keep all my verse—mostly they're just collections of images. Very seldom do I jot down a story, and the reason is I try to hide from my stories. I'm afraid if I tell them to myself, I've removed the pressure from telling them to others, but also then I'm writing to a template that I don't want. It's just how I'm wired. My friend Tracy Kidder needs to tell his stories repeatedly. I know, because we drive to the Keys every year together, and it's a long drive.

On occasions, a finished story started out as a poem, and usually it's because I can't figure out how to make a poem work. Characters start appearing, and something happens that makes me realize that now I'll never control this poem. I would like to think that when that happens accidentally, that it kind of puts poetry DNA in a story's genes, but it's only by accident that it happens. But I'm all for accident. I saw a story on fashion—the clothes were really weird, big baggy things—and the designer said that the way she designs clothes is she waits to see some kind of accident happen, and if it's interesting, she follows that accident.


## EDWARD P. JONES

For *The Known World*, I started thinking about the novel and I just sort of took my own time. I didn't have any sort of deadline. And I didn't have a problem with sustaining any inspiration. It was always there. I took ten years or so thinking it up, and I only had twelve pages of hard copy. So when I first sat down to write, the first draft took two and a half months. That's the physical part of writing, but the ten years of thinking it through counts as writing as well.

I don't have any other novels stuffed in a desk drawer. Floating around in my head, perhaps.


## JOHN DALTON

*Heaven Lake* spun out of an offer that was actually made to me when I was living in Taiwan in the 1980s. I was out to dinner one night with other foreign English teachers in Taiwan and we were approached by a Taiwanese businessman. We drank a lot of beer, and as it got late, he had this proposition for us all. The previous summer he had gone to mainland China to open up a factory and had met a woman whom he described as the most beautiful woman in China. He wanted to marry her, she wanted to marry him. But at the time there was no way politically for this to happen. So he made a standing offer to anyone at the table that he would pay $10,000 if one of us would go to China, find the woman, marry her—because an American or Canadian could marry someone from China—then return the bride to him in Taiwan and then get a divorce.

So, in truth, this guy was flaky and drunk, but he gave me an idea that I knew right away I could build a novel around. So that's the setup for the plot. Thematically it's about faith. The main character is a Christian volunteer who makes a big mistake and agrees to take on this journey across China. It's an especially complex proposition for Vincent, because he's a Christian missionary from the Midwest and the situation forces him into complexities he had previously not even considered.

## SHIRLEY HAZZARD

I've lived with *The Great Fire* all my grown-up life. It was my experience in the Far East, but it's "material" that waited for me a long time. I knew I would use it eventually, and I began to think about it as a book more than twenty years ago when I finished *The Transit of Venus*. And then I began to write it in the 1980s, and some chapters were published in *The New Yorker* then, but quite a lot of the draft material I discarded. I didn't think it was developed enough. I had to convalesce from discarding those things, so I wrote a book about the Waldheim case. I saw it would be pushed under the UN rug again; the book is called *Continents of Truth*. And then came a time in my life where my husband, who is considerably older than I, needed me more. His memory was failing, so in his last year I could only work sporadically on my long-gestated novel. I still felt it passionately and I still thought about it constantly. And that's when I did the memoir of Graham Greene. One of my pleasures in writing the memoir of

Graham was remembering my life with my husband. Graham wasn't exactly an excuse, but I liked having a chance to give a context to the way we lived.

And then I thought, now I'll finish my novel. It was a great consolation.


## FRANCES ITANI

I did not know until I visited the school for the deaf that I would be writing a book about a deaf child (and woman). My own grandmother did become deaf when she was a baby, but my character, Grania, becomes deaf at the age of five, because I wanted her to have a good understanding of language before her deafness. It was in 1996 that I decided to write this book. My grandmother died in 1987 when she was eighty-nine, so she was not around, unfortunately, to answer my questions. However, I was very close to her and remembered many things about her behavior and mannerisms, and I used a few examples of these in my book. I think most books begin as a surprise to the writer, and in 1996, when I became hooked on the idea for *Deafening*, it was certainly a surprise to me.

I did it out of absolute love for my grandmother, and that's what kept me going, because six years is a long time to work on a book. And when I was right smack in the middle of this book and wondering if I'd ever finish, I would call up my love for my grandmother and keep going.


## MARGOT LIVESEY

*Eva Moves the Furniture* is really a love song to my mother. It was a very conscious decision to put her name in the title, to use her real name, and to use everything I knew about her, which was not a great deal. But the parts about the character's relationship with the supernatural, about being visited by poltergeists, and seeing people who are not visible to most other people, come directly from the handful of stories that I have about my mother. Several people recorded the presence of poltergeists, and it was a joke among her acquaintances that when Eva was around, poltergeists would visit and move the furniture. And the story about her seeing other people who were not visible to most other people comes from someone who had what in Scotland we call "second sight," or being fey.

When I started the novel in 1987, those stories about the supernatural were one of the main reasons I wanted to write the novel. However, as soon became apparent, writing about otherworldly matters in the white Anglo-Saxon tradition is a peculiarly complicated thing to do, and I found myself struggling to bridge the gap between credulity and skepticism, which I think informs how many people regard such occurrences. Most people that I talked to turned out to have had a number of supernatural experiences themselves, whether it was a moment of telepathy or coincidence or a sense of intimacy with someone who's dead or far away. At the same time, most people express scorn or skepticism for other people's stories. So finding a way to say how Eva glimpses a world beyond normal appearance and yet not offend my more skeptical readers was a real challenge.

In writing the last chapter of *Eva Moves the Furniture*— which I wrote almost in a single sitting—I did have the experience of somehow being in contact with her, and although I'm the kind of person who revises things endlessly, I knew when I had written that chapter that I was not going to change it substantially.

## TIM PARKS

I actually threw away a whole book about five years ago. The hardest thing as a novelist, at least for me, is the moment, after you've written, say, twenty or thirty pages, when you have to commit to the book. You wonder: Do I really believe in this plot, these people? Is it going to work, can I give the next year to it? And often I'll waver there for months, reading and rereading and thinking, does the world really need this stuff? (The answer, alas, is no, but that's hardly the point.) I'd like to say that one gets better at understanding what is the right thing to do, but it's really not the case for me. It's always an act of faith when I finally go for it, and it's often with some amazement, two hundred pages on, that I grasp the last part of the novel and how it's going to work. All of a sudden, it seems inevitable.

## JHUMPA LAHIRI

The promise of success has never inspired me to write, and a lack of it will never keep me from it. I think writing does get harder as you go on, but only because you're setting up bigger challenges for yourself. I work to meet my own expectations, and not anybody else's. Success doesn't make writing any easier, and for me it hasn't made it any harder, either. It's always hard. When I'm at my desk, I don't think about how my work is perceived or received. You have to approach every new work with humility, and a sense of awe, and you have to remain humble, in a way, to that act, to that process.

# Who Reads This Stuff?

## *How Writers Think About Audience—and Reviewers*

Unlike actors and musicians, jugglers and circus clowns, writers don't do their work in front of an audience. If they write a sentence so taut and beautiful it makes them weep, no one is around to applaud—or even notice.

Then one day, a book is out, and the solitary writer is reading in front of strangers, being asked about the kind of notebook she uses, and wondering where in the world the reviewer got the idea that the father in the novel was a gay woman. Suddenly, there's an audience.

Many writers here say it's surprising to see how their work is interpreted, but they also realize they have absolutely no control over it. The book takes on a life of its own.

This is one reason most say they can't think of audience, or reviewers, when they are in the middle of writing. Creation is individual.

But a few writers have people who somehow typify the audience they hope to entice, entertain, enthrall with their work. Margot Livesey thinks of her two adopted sisters in Scotland and hopes her work will live up to the desires and expectations of those inveterate readers. Walter Mosley quite purposefully continues writing mysteries because the genre allows him to introduce political themes to a wider audience, some of whom might not otherwise be interested. A. S. Byatt says that she used to write for herself and the ghost of Henry James, and then *Possession* became a best seller. It turned upside down her ideas about what a contemporary audience is willing to read.


## MARTIN AMIS

After a while, you stop defending yourself and go more into attack. I use the boastful mode. I could give you a big spiel about the cultural wars I seem to have wandered into. Basically, I'll just say that my stuff, my writing, makes people a little crazy sometimes and unleashes rivalrous and sometimes murderous passions.

It does please me a little bit. You know, there's the Norman Mailer line where you don't want to be understood too quickly. You don't want to be patted on the back and pigeonholed and then—on to the next thing. But it's gone beyond a joke in England, and every time I have a book out now signifies a new low in the so-called literary journalistic world.

I have been outflanked by the culture. I am now seen as a drawling Oxonian and a genetic elitist who took over the family firm. People subconsciously think that I was born in 1922, wrote *Lucky Jim* when I was seven, and will live for at least a century. This feels odd to me, because my father was an "angry young man" and helped democratize the British novel. I'm not a toff. I'm a yob.

I once wrote, in *The Information*, that an Englishman wouldn't bother to attend a reading even if the author in question was his favorite living writer, and also his long-lost brother—even if the reading was taking place next door. Whereas Americans go out and do things. But Meeting the Author, for me, is Meeting the Reader. Some of the little exchanges that take place over the signing table I find very fortifying: They make up for some of the other stuff you get.


## A. S. BYATT

Before I wrote *Possession*, I was often criticized for being erudite or complicated, and I used to say, "I write for myself or for Henry James." I had a very clear idea of the ghost of Henry James as moral support. However, when *Possession* became a best seller, I got so many letters from so many kinds of readers that I decided there are readers who can be interested in almost anything—including erudition—as long as you also tell a story. I enjoy meeting readers because writing is very lonely—and I enjoy being alone—but I am constantly amazed to meet people who have read and liked my books.

American editors speak of some imaginary person, The American Reader, who will not understand things. I have formed the view that they are speaking of somebody who would never buy books anyway. America is full of readers of all different sorts who love books in many different ways, and I keep meeting them. And I think editors should look after them, and make less effort to please people who don't actually like books.


## STUART DYBEK

I think you have to be careful underestimating the working class's commitment to art. The house I grew up in had only

*Reader's Digest.* But with people in the working class who do get a relationship to the arts, it's almost religious in its intensity. There's sometimes a fervor to a working-class artist, and I think working-class readers have an extraordinarily intense connection to it, because they haven't grown up with that particular kind of art.

## JOYCE CAROL OATES

When we begin as writers, our hopes are very modest. Simply to be published is a very astonishing phenomenon, and we tend to be very grateful for any kind of early encouragement. I was extremely fortunate because one of my first stories when I was nineteen was published in a national magazine, *Mademoiselle.* And so I had immediate readership at an unexpectedly young age. I don't really think of an audience when I write because the story on which I'm working is usually, to me, unique, and I have no idea to whom it would be appropriate.

## MAUREEN HOWARD

I want to tell my stories. I don't think of the best-educated reader at all; I don't think of it on a scale of 1 to 10. I want to appeal to the reader and make everything quite accessible. I do love language, and the rhythm of sentences and the rhythm of paragraphs. I think that there's a lot of good fiction being written that is not in any way dumbed down. And the other thing is, to go back to an old story, I think if you try to write down—if you say, I'm going to write a real dumbo murder mystery or thriller—I think if you don't have that talent, I don't think you can do it.

## SHIRLEY HAZZARD

Though *The Great Fire* has gotten some attention, I don't feel I've been rediscovered. I've been here all the time. This is like saying that Dr. Livingstone discovered Africa—the people were there all the time. I am very happy that this book has come out and it has such wonderful readers. It's a great happiness to me to be back on the scene in that way with a novel, because I love fiction and I never want to write anything else. I'm very happy that the book has appeared, and that many people have liked it.

## MARGOT LIVESEY

Reading saved my life when I was growing up. In my rather solitary childhood, I was extremely dependent on the library. I grew up mostly reading these wonderful Victorian novels where you can completely enter into the lives of the characters. And that still remains one of my deep ambitions as a writer—to make my readers feel as if the people in my books are like neighbors or friends about whom you can have opinions and arguments, about whom you can approve or disapprove, their lives becoming an extension, if you will, of your own life. And I would also say that I have two very hardworking adopted sisters in Scotland who are also passionate readers, and when I'm writing, I always have in mind my desire to keep them awake a little longer when they come home to read after their long days. They do read my work; they're both wonderful, generous readers of my work.

I think that I've always believed that literature could achieve its higher aims while still being entertaining and enjoyable, that it's possible to write really good literary novels that are still a pleasure to read, and entertaining.


## ELIZABETH GRAVER

I don't have a "target" audience in mind in any specific way. I have a few trusted readers who see the book in pieces, at various stages: My friend the writer Lauren Slater sees it first, then other close friends, some of them writers, others not; then my parents, my sister, and my husband.

It then slowly makes its way out into wider circles. My editor, Jennifer Barth, is an amazing editor, and I think of her as an audience as I write in that I trust her taste and also trust her to help me shape my novels. If I had to try to define who my ideal, wider audience would be, it would be readers who admire the work of contemporary writers I deeply admire. That list might contain (among many other names) the following: Alice Munro, Toni Morrison, Howard Norman, Julia Glass, Margot Livesey, Michael Ondaatje, Grace Paley, Gish Jen, William Trevor. If people who loved their books were also to love my own, I would be thrilled.

During the actual writing, though, I suppose I'm writing for myself, in that I'm inside the world I'm creating, not thinking about being read so much as getting words down, one by one, on the page, until they form into sentences, then paragraphs, then chapters.


## WALTER MOSLEY

In one way, you could see a difference between genre fiction and "literary fiction." But really there's an umbrella called "literary quality." Everything that falls beneath that umbrella is literary fiction. And those books that do not are not. But a book that falls under the umbrella of literary quality could be a "literary" book, or science fiction, or romance, or thriller. Because what defines literary quality is the quality of the writing, not the subject, not the genre, and not even the author.

The best thing politically I like about the mystery genre is that if you write a book about a Chicano farmworker in central California and his trials and tribulations, the only people who read it are people who are that or who are interested in that world. But if a person is murdered on that farm, and you have a Chicano detective coming into that world and describing that world in order to solve the crime, then you have a much broader audience willing to find out about that world because of the genre. It's one reason why I keep doing it.

## ANTHONY DOERR

I would certainly not be upset, or I would be perfectly content, if someone wanted to call *About Grace* a thriller, a psychic thriller, or any kind of thriller. At the same time, I never set out to write a thriller. In fact, the only bad review comment I've gotten so far is that the book is too long, and not enough happens in it. Reviewers have said some really nice things, but some are saying it's too long, and I would say that's the opposite of a thriller. I suppose I would not be surprised if someone called it a patient book. I've been on this reading tour and I've seen it on the science-fiction shelf, and it surprised me. I'm happy to see it there, especially if it gets me readers I wouldn't necessarily get. But it's not how I conceived

of it. I think those are more marketing terms. I never think
of those when I'm trying to create a story.

## GISH JEN

Being published in China has been a wonderful experience
for me. Especially when I was writing my first novel, *Typical
American*, I could not imagine any audience, much less an
international audience. So it's a thrill, so many years later, to
have Chinese readers come to me and say, "You really understand the Chinese." They always tell me the characters are
"typical Chinese."

## MARIE ARANA

It is a challenge being both a published writer and a critic,
but you know—how can I grouse about any of it when
both roles give me such joy? I feel very fortunate to live this
double life. I grew up bicultural, and now I guess I'm bipro-
fessional. It's a bit awkward, but comfortable at the same
time.

In truth, there are a lot of pitfalls for the critic who writes.
There are so many writers out there whose books have been
taken to task on the pages of *Book World*: Who knows who
might want to take a potshot at the editor?

And I'm afraid I fairly hamstrung my publisher about
publicity. I have lots of rules about blurbs. (None. I can't
afford to have famous authors' quotes on my books. It would
look like a lot of mutual backslapping, even if it weren't so.)
I have lots of worries about overpublicizing, being too much
in the limelight. That wouldn't look very good either for a

book editor who should be looking after everyone else's books.

But, in the main, I feel very lucky to be where I am.

## CHARLES BAXTER

When I first wrote "Saul and Patsy Are Getting Comfortable in Michigan" in 1983, I ended the story with an automobile accident. (It was an amateurish way to end a story—you can't end a short story with an accident because it never looks accidental; it looks arranged by the writer.) A month or so after the story appeared, a large woman at a Detroit literary soirée came up to me, grabbed my lapel, and started shaking me. "You have your nerve," she said, "killing off that nice couple like that." I said, "They're not dead!" I suppose she had intimidated me and caused me to see the error of my ways. In any case, I told her that you could roll a car in Michigan without anything happening to you—it's very flat—and in the next Saul and Patsy story, I had the two of them crawling out of the car and walking to a nearby house, to call for help. That was the beginning of the series, and I decided to turn the whole thing into a novel when an older writer said to me, "I don't think we've seen the end of Gordy Himmelman." He was right; we hadn't. It was Gordy who took us the rest of the way into the novel.

At first, women seemed to like *The Feast of Love* better than men did, but I've been hearing recently from men's groups that they've been reading it and, for the most part, liking it, so apparently the novel does not divide people along gender lines in quite the way I thought it might.

The truth is that I'm never sure how any of my books will

be received, and because I can be thin-skinned, I try not to read too many reviews when one of my books first comes out.

## ART SPIEGELMAN

Some reviewers thought I was just padding out *In the Shadow of No Towers* with an appendix. When you're with pages that are each a quarter of an inch thick, it doesn't seem to me one could or would need any more padding. I thought of the old Sunday comics in the back as a second tower, next to my own pages, that brought out a theme in the work that had to do with the nature of ephemera. That is, when two monumental, 110-story-high towers prove to be ephemeral, when a two-hundred-plus-year-old democratic republic seems to be so fragile, perhaps the ephemeral, like the old Sunday comics born in New York right next door to the Twin Towers, can be seen as monumental, as art, as something that can inform our current culture.

## CAROLYN PARKHURST

Some people seem to absolutely love my first book, *The Dogs of Babel*, and others absolutely hate it, and I'm not sure why that is. I like your theory that it's due to the book's emotional content, but I think there are probably other factors at play as well, one of which is just taste. There's no book that absolutely *everyone* likes. I think that, in the case of my book, because there was a lot of advance publicity, some people expected the book to be something other than it was, and high expectations can lead to disappointment. But it's one of my greatest thrills when someone tells me that they were affected by the book, and I've been lucky enough to have that happen a lot.

## MARISHA PESSL

Certainly one of the surprising truths of having a book published is realizing that your book is as open to interpretation as an abstract painting. People bring their own beliefs and attitudes to your work, which is thrilling and surprising at the same time.

## PAUL AUSTER

I would never tell anyone to read my books. It's not my job to do that. But all my life as a writer, I've had very disparate responses, contradictory responses, to the work I do. Some people love it and other people simply despise it. I get the best reviews and the worst reviews of any writer I know, and there's nothing, nothing in the world I can do about it. I would of course prefer that everyone love what I do, but I've been doing this work long enough to know that that's never going to happen.

# Good Writers Borrow,
# Great Writers Steal

## *The Writers Whom Writers Love, and Why*

It was T. S. Eliot who coined this famous phrase—the same writer who, paradoxically, so strived to "make it new." Or maybe not so paradoxically. Writers take certain authors and books into their hearts, but they cannot ever mimic them— just as Bolognese sauces cooked with the same ingredients will taste differently depending on the chef. What comes out is the writers' own voices, their own stories.

The writers whom other writers talk about in this chapter as influences are an eclectic mix of the realist and surrealist, political and apolitical, classic and brand new. Looking at their lists of favorites, one could not necessarily predict the type of work authors end up writing. Charles Baxter and Flaubert? Pam Houston and D. H. Lawrence? And yet, one can see the connection and understand better what the contemporary writer is getting at in his work (because there *is* something over-the-top and Lawrencian about the passion Houston's saucy narrators have for cowboys, and Baxter's easy, Midwestern style reveals itself, on second glance, to be as controlled as Flaubert's).

Perhaps, for writers at least, literature should be taught in reverse chronological order. We come up with more pairings: Auster and Cervantes, Edward P. Jones and James Joyce, Gish Jen and Jane Austen. How much sense they all make. What an interesting lens through which to consider current work. And look at how powerful is the cord that snakes back and connects one writer to the next, to the next, to the next.

T. S. Eliot again: "No poet, no artist of any art, has his complete meaning alone."

## RICHARD BAUSCH

The three writers are Shakespeare, Tolstoy, and Chekhov. They're the best—there's nobody better. They're the ones who get my motor running. They write about human distress. "Sing of human unsuccess/In a rapture of distress" (from W. H. Auden).

## PAUL AUSTER

The list is too long to enumerate today, but I'll give a few names: Montaigne, Shakespeare, Cervantes, Dickens, Dostoyevsky, Tolstoy, Hawthorne, Melville, Thoreau, Kafka, Beckett, Joyce, Celine, Fitzgerald, Faulkner, etc.

These days, in the United States, I'm very fond of Don DeLillo's work. Robert Coover, García-Márquez, Kundera.

The last novel I read is the new translation into English of *Don Quixote*, by Edith Grossman, which I enjoyed very much. *Don Quixote* is probably my favorite novel of all time, and I've read it at least five times.

## E. L. DOCTOROW

It's a long list of writers from the past who've influenced me. The great nineteenth-century writers in England, Dickens, George Eliot, and, earlier than that, Fielding; in France, Flaubert, Stendahl; in Russia, Tolstoy, Dostoyevsky, Chekhov. Nothing unusual about this. In America, Hawthorne, Melville, Mark Twain, Dreiser, Scott Fitzgerald.

A book I wish I could have written is Cervantes's *Don Quixote*.

Add Dos Passos to that list. Dos Passos enlarged the possibilities of the novel for all of us who came after. He did separate his historical passages and his documentary materials from the rest of the fiction, but we brought down that wall.

Among the great twentieth-century writers, Woolf's obviously right up there. The work of hers that impresses me most is *Mrs. Dalloway*. That's an extraordinary book. She wanted to write a novel without a subject and render life without a plot, and I think she succeeds. It's unfortunate that all this attention to her life has risen between readers and her work.

## DAN CHAON

I can give a really long list, but I'll give a shorter list. Two authors who have been major influences on my writing are Alice Munro and Russell Banks. Other writers I love are David Means, Lynda Barry, Michael Chabon, Denis Johnson, John Edgar Wideman. And then, in terms of more classic literature, I love Dickens, and Nabokov, and Borges, and Elizabeth Bowen. I love Edwardian ghost stories. And Raymond Carver. He's getting a bad rep from some people, and I'm going to stick by the guy. I'm tired of people bad-mouthing Ray Carver.

## GISH JEN

Among classic writers, certainly Shakespeare and Jane Austen are very important to me. *The Love Wife* is a hybrid form. It's somewhere between drama and the novel and was inspired partly by Naipaul's work, which is also hybrid. I'm also endlessly impressed with his terrible candor, which I so admire.

I haven't been so much influenced by Chinese writers writing in Chinese, although I will say that Mao Dun, who was one of the great early twentieth-century writers, is a distant cousin and did study with my grandfather. So there may be some influence there of which I'm unaware. In terms of the Chinese-American writers, I have mostly written against writers such as Maxine Hong Kingston, having no choice. I adore her as a person, but she was, in Harold Bloom-ian terms, a strong poet that I had to throw over in order to write at all.

## PAM HOUSTON

I think different writers inspire us at different times in our lives. At one time I said I was the illegitimate child of the unlikely and certainly unhappy marriage between D. H. Lawrence and Willa Cather. When I was in graduate school, I devoured Richard Ford, Russell Banks, Lorrie Moore, Ron Carlson. These days, I take a lot of inspiration from contemporary poets. Two books I've been reading and rereading all year are Franz Wright's *Walking to Martha's Vineyard*, and Mark Doty's *School of the Arts*. Most recently, Mary Gaitskill's

*Veronica* rocked my universe in a way that will show up in my writing somehow.

I think the writers I love best fall into two categories: writers who have a similar vision or project to mine, and writers that I'm so amazed by what they do I can't even imagine. It's the in-between ones that fall through the cracks.

A couple of people who jump to mind whose work might be similar to my own are Lorrie Moore, Amy Bloom, Amy Hempel, Richard Ford (though he might not agree!). My favorite writers at the moment are Alice Munro, Toni Morrison, and J. M. Coetzee. I'm not sure I'd say they mine similar territory, not specifically. But what I tried to learn from them is how to represent the experience of being alive in all its complication and multiplicity.


## MICHAEL CUNNINGHAM

Both Wallace Stevens and Virginia Woolf are part of my consciousness, as are Pamela Lee and *Queer Eye for the Straight Guy*. I write from everything that influences me, Woolf and Stevens being two of the more presentable. I am obviously interested in the notion of making art out of art, because I feel that art should be honored as a living thing. And I think that if we take art seriously, we understand that it is material every bit as rich and viable as our personal experience.


## WALTER MOSLEY

I like Márquez, certainly. So many of the authors I love are gone. Zola, Langston Hughes, Chester Himes, so many of the hard-boiled writers, Dashiell Hammett, James M. Cain. And then of course we come into the modern day, and you have people such as Edna O'Brien, Toni Morrison, John Edgar Wideman. But I don't read books because of who wrote them. I begin reading and continue reading books because I enjoy the book itself. Many good authors have written many bad books. And many mediocre writers have at least one gem to their name. You just pick up books and start reading them. See if you like them. If you don't like it, pick up another book.

## DOREEN BAINGANA

African writers I like: Ben Okri from Nigeria, who wrote *The Famished Road*. His short story collection, *Incidents at the Shrine*, is excellent. I have had the wonderful fortune to meet some new writers through the Caine Prize for African Writing. I was a finalist and I met young writers from Kenya, Zimbabwe, and Nigeria, and each year the Caine Prize has an anthology of the work of the winners. (If people go to www.caineprize.com, they can get a list of the winners and they can look for their writing.)

I have found a great curiosity and interest among the people I know, white and black, in my work, and I think that people just don't know about the writers. People are interested in writing and reading from other cultures—if they knew more about these writers, they would read them.

My favorite writer ever: This may be a standard choice, but Toni Morrison. Her book *Beloved* had the political, the personal, history, and it's also a great love story. It has everything.

## RUSSELL BANKS

What I like to read varies enormously, depending on what I'm working on at the time. Right now, I'm writing a novel

that is set in 1936 in upstate New York, and it involves—in
ways I haven't yet figured out—the Spanish Civil War. So I've
been reading George Orwell's *Homage to Catalonia*, and
Hemingway's writing on the Spanish Civil War, John Dos
Passos, and others. And also because I want it to be a short
novel, a kind of fable, I've been reading short novels, such as
*Bridge of San Luis Rey*, Henry James's *The Lesson of the Master*,
Tolstoy's *The Devil*, and so on.

## ANTHONY DOERR

Rick Bass—I always start with him. Just the risks he'll take,
the way he manages to build narratives around landscape and
make them unconventional. I love that. Andrea Barrett. Her
book, *Ship Fever*, was really important to me when I was
learning how to write. I just read a book called *Hunger*, by
Elise Blackwell; it's excellent, about the siege of Leningrad.
It's just a slim, beautiful, quick book—I highly recommend it.

The kind of obvious: Fitzgerald and Faulkner, I just
devoured everything they wrote for a couple of years. Rachel
Carson. Not only *Silent Spring* but *The Sea Around Us* is an
awesome book. Even though she doesn't write narrative, she
didn't write novels, her whole legacy—that prose can change
the world, that prose can affect people—was so powerful to
me, and still is.

## ANDREA LEVY

I tend to like books rather than writers. A top-ten list of my
favorites always goes on in my head. I'll give you the first
three. In at number three is Philip Roth and *The Human
Stain*. A brilliant piece of work, breathtaking. Just fantastic.

At number two is *English Passengers*, by Matthew Kneale. I like this book because it tells a story, a ripping good story, at the same time as giving you information and education about what was happening with the British Empire in Australia during the nineteenth century. So that's my sort of book. And in at number one is *The Remains of the Day*, by Kazuo Ishiguro. For a writer, I think it's a gem of a book. There's not one single word out of place. I think it's a real jewel, and a real interesting story, again with a historical element.

I love books that make you feel once you've read them that they've added to the sum total of who you are. That you've learned something or you've been taken somewhere that was really worth going to, because you understand something better now. I never read a book of fiction until I was twenty-three; I only read nonfiction because I thought you couldn't learn anything from fiction.

I read a book called *The Women's Room*, by Marilyn French. And it was the first time that I'd read a book that spoke to me, entertained me, told me stories in a way that changed the way I felt about something. So it was a profoundly moving thing. I hadn't realized books could do that. I'd grown up with having to do examinations in the British classics, and having to try to read Dickens and Charlotte Brontë. And I thought that was all that books were about. They were about hard work. And now I don't think that.

I didn't start writing fiction until I was in my early thirties. But I became an avid reader from the age of twenty-three, and now I'm trying to go back over all those classics that I didn't get around to reading for school. I'm currently reading *Middlemarch* by George Eliot. It's a fantastic book, absolutely fantastic. As a writer, she was absolutely at her peak, and she seemed like she was enjoying it as she was writing it. It's wonderful.

But I do have a writer I really like, and that's Ian McEwan. I think he's an absolutely fantastic storyteller. And also a very clear, interesting, and concise writer. I like that in writing. Not too baggy.

## CHARLES BAXTER

Favorites: the Russians, particularly Tolstoy and Chekhov and Bulgakov. Always Flaubert. . . . The more I try to answer this question, the more I find it unanswerable, because it turns into a laundry list, a list that is always being revised. I always like to say, however, that I have learned more from Katherine Anne Porter's story "Noon Wine" than I have from almost any other literary source.

If you read my story "Kiss Away," in *Believers*, you'll see how I adapted the structure of "Noon Wine" for my own purposes—including the arrival, two-thirds of the way through, of a stranger whose motives are suspect and perhaps dangerous. There's more, but I need to keep my professional honor intact.

## MARISHA PESSL

I think every writer has a book that haunts him or her, and, on some level, every book you write is a reaction to it. *Lolita* is that book for me. Nabokov's love of wordplay, descriptive detail, artfully complex plots, and his themes of obsession and lost love, are inspiring.

In *Special Topics in Calamity Physics*, I was interested in how the books we read, those that are life-changing, stop relying on the author and become our own in a way that has nothing to do with the character or the plot. For example, when I think of *The Catcher in the Rye*, I think back to my circumstances in reading that. I was visiting my uncle in Venezuela. I remember my personal experiences, and that almost eclipses the plot of that book.

Along these same lines, the chapter titles [which are also the titles of famous books or movies] take on new and often humorous connotations based on the events in each chapter. Each chapter, you could say, contains a tiny mystery as to why Blue, the protagonist of *Special Topics in Calamity Physics,* names it what she did. Some are obvious, others more obscure.

As for my own academic background, I was an English literature major in school, and, like Blue, I spent my childhood reading the classics. My mother read the classics out loud to my sister and me, and that is how I first experienced *Crime and Punishment, The Woman in White*, etc.

In terms of contemporary writers, I like Michael Chabon, Jeffrey Eugenides, Ian McEwan. I like Charles D'Ambrosio—his *Dead Fish Museum* is great.

I don't want to be compared to anyone. I think every novelist wants to forge his or her own tiny path.

## MAUREEN HOWARD

Dickens, of course. The range of Dickens, as he got deeper and deeper in his later work, and the way in which he could weave separate strains of his story together, is terribly important to me. We think of Dickens as enormously accessible, and he is, but in his later work he is also very demanding that we put together the stories. It's wonderful when you think about what he does in *Bleak House*, that he separates out different stories for voices to interact, which is something I like to do.

Of course I use an awful lot of Melville. *Moby-Dick* demands a lot of the reader, but it's an adventure for the reader. It's a book he wrote first as an adventure; in a letter to Hawthorne, he said he couldn't write in that way anymore. He sat down and took the whaling adventure and rewrote the entire book, because he knew he could not write another whaling adventure and not write all the other stories that spilled out from it, stories of art, of myth, scenes from Shakespeare, an amazing adventure that you're on. Which Bel [the protagonist in *The Silver Screen*] doesn't really get. She doesn't quite ever make it all the way through.

Then of course the thing about Melville, his career was such a failure after the to-do of the early novels. *Moby-Dick* was a terrible failure. The publisher didn't want much to do with him after that.

I have just been looking at Edith Wharton, and *The House of Mirth* and *The Age of Innocence* are wonderful books, and Virginia Woolf, of course Virginia Woolf, *To the Lighthouse*, and the book she wrote just before she committed suicide, *Between the Acts*. It spans all of history. She does something I reach for.


SHIRLEY HAZZARD

Graham Greene taught me about writing, long before I ever met him. In 1947 at Christmas, when I was living in Hong Kong with my parents, I asked for a Christmas present, for a new novel of his that had just come out, *The Heart of the*

*Matter.* I was sixteen at the time, and I had read novels of Graham's before, because from the time I was about twelve or so I was aware of his existence as a writer, especially because there were already films of his books that he called entertainment. When I asked for this book for Christmas, I was by then beginning to grow up, and it had a new effect on me. It was the fact of being able to write like that in a clear way about what was close to one's own relatively contemporary feelings, and very direct about the emotions a sensitive reader would feel. If I had to choose one novel of Graham Greene's as his best, I would still choose *The Heart of the Matter.*

I wasn't a writer then. But it affected me in that I appreciated this thing that I was seeing fresh, because at that age one is changing. And I understood what this was, the difficulty he had in love and trying to be truthful and trying to be true to himself. It's certainly his kindest book. There is more human kindness in it than in most of the books. He also came to dislike the book because people felt that it was more accessible in a sense. It speaks more directly to responsiveness in human beings rather than difficulty.

## THISBE NISSEN

I read *Moby-Dick* for the first time in the most wonderful way. Marilynne Robinson, who's a professor at the Iowa Writers' Workshop, whenever she teaches a class at the university, she also teaches it at her church. And a couple of springs ago, she lost her room at the church, so we wound up doing the class in my living room. So every Thursday night, a whole group of people—Marilynne and mostly workshop

grads who are still around town and then community members from the church—all convened at my house for a *Moby-
Dick* seminar that lasted all semester. How incredibly glorious
to have Marilynne and this group of intellectual, curious
people come and sit in your living room with your cats
climbing all over them and talk about *Moby-Dick*. My
strongest feeling when I finally started reading *Moby-Dick*,
which had always been hanging over me, because I'd never
read it, was I came into class the second week and said,
"Nobody ever told me that *Moby-Dick* was funny!" The
absurdity of some things, and he's got such a sly sense of
humor. It's marvelous.

## TOD GOLDBERG

I must say that my very first inspiration was my brother Lee,
who has been publishing novels since I was nine or ten. He
went out and did it first and sort of paved the way for me
in many regards. Outside of the family, I've been most
inspired by folks such as Richard Ford, who was the first
writer I read in college who made me realize that Stephen
King was not the foremost chronicler of the human condition; and Robertson Davies, whose novel *Fifth Business*
made me take notice of how language and emotion create
character; and Richard Russo, who is able to make the
minutiae of life the stuff of Shakespearean drama. But I'm
also inspired by more contemporary writers, such as Mary
Yukari Waters, who I believe is writing the best short fiction, period, of anyone in America; and Scott Phillips, who
I think is writing tremendous crime fiction; and Mary
Roach, who makes me wish I could write nonfiction with
her flair and wit and importance.

## FRANCES ITANI

I would say that I learned a great deal from Chekhov, also from the letters and diaries of Virginia Woolf. And I read many contemporary writers. People whose work I've read recently are Kaye Gibbons, Helen Dunmore, Charles Frazier, and many, many others.

Currently, I've just read a collection of short stories by Penelope Lively called *Beyond the Blue Mountains*, which has great wit. Alistair MacLeod is one of my favorites. He won the IMPAC Dublin Award [for *No Great Mischief* ] and should certainly be read. I also enjoy Sebastian Faulks. Arthur Miller—I go back to his plays every once in a while. If I were to recommend, I would say read Seamus Heaney for sure. And Kate Grenville, the Australian writer. Her book, *The Idea of Perfection*, is one of my favorites.

## EDWARD P. JONES

There are too many people that I admire to mention people. As far as my first book, *Lost in the City*, I had read James Joyce's *Dubliners*, and I was quite taken with what he had done with Dublin. So I set out to do the same thing for Washington, DC. I went away to college and people have a very narrow idea of what Washington is like. They don't know that it's a place of neighborhoods, for example, and I set out to give a better picture of what the city is like—the other city.

## MARIE ARANA

My heroes and models are Nabokov, Conrad, Flannery O'Connor, E. E. Cummings. I feel their writing so deeply it

sometimes amazes me, because they write about such different things.

For me, it's as much the care writers take with their language as it is the story itself.

I was very moved by Geraldine Brooks's *March*. And I am
still reeling from Alice McDermott's *After This*. I wouldn't say
we occupy the same territory at all, though.

I'm just so glad they're there and doing what it is they do.

## 15

# I Knew Him When . . .

## *When Writers Realized They*
## *Were Going to Be Writers*

After reading the anecdotes in this chapter, one thing seems clear: A person doesn't "become" a writer. You don't go to school for it, you don't get a writing job, you don't quit a job to become a writer. Making yourself a better writer, making it a vocation (not a profession), making a series of decisions (usually bad financial ones) that will give you more time to write—those are clearer forks in the road. But when does a writer become a writer? Never, and always.

Some writers here say they have wanted to be writers since they were young children—"Since I was old enough to form letters," Elizabeth Graver says. And others were writing away in their twenties and thirties or forties but not allowing themselves to say they were writers, not wanting to be presumptuous. The point at which they began to call themselves writers was often long past when they had actually become one.

So in retrospect, Marisha Pessl now sees that she was a writer even as a child because she was writing stories that turned into novels, and Joanna Scott was a writer once she was writing poems, and Michael Cunningham was a writer even when he was writing but making money only by bartending.

So when did they become writers? When they began to write.

## EDWARD P. JONES

You don't really become a writer. You're always a writer. If you write a story today, and you get up tomorrow and start another story, all the expertise that you put into the first story doesn't transfer over automatically to the second story. You're always starting at the bottom of the mountain. So you're always becoming a writer. You're never really arriving. Whatever nice things people say about *The Known World*, I can't take that tomorrow and start a new book. I can't put that into a creative bank. You think about all those people who write all those wonderful books, and then number nine or ten is horrible. Where did all that expertise go?

## ELIZABETH GRAVER

I've been writing stories since I was old enough to form letters, and if you had asked me at the age of six what I wanted to be when I grew up, I'd have said, "A writer." My parents both taught English, so our house was full of books, but I have also always been a person (like Anna in *Awake*, I suppose) with a vivid imaginary life or dream world. As a child, I wrote, drew, played elaborate "pretend games" in the woods with my best friend. When I got older, and it became embarrassing to play with dolls, writing took over. I wrote stories in college; took a few years off from school but kept writing; went to grad school; kept writing . . . I've just always done it. Right out of college, I had a writers group that served as my "audience"; that was incredibly helpful, a way to get feedback and not feel like I was going at it alone. We met on and off for some ten years. The other members of that group (Audrey Schulman, Lauren Slater, Pagan Kennedy) have now all published many books. When we first got together, we were fresh out of college and just knew that this was what we wanted to try to do. We were stubborn, we had grit, we supported each other. It was an amazing time.

## CAROLYN PARKHURST

I've wanted to be a writer for as long as I can remember (except for a brief time in the second grade when I wanted to be an inventor, which I guess isn't all that different). I was always writing stories as a child, and there was never really anything else I could imagine doing for a living. I didn't necessarily know how to go about it, of course. I majored in English in college, then worked in a bookstore for three years while I took writing classes and wrote stories, but it often felt as if I was never going to get to the point when I could really call myself a writer. Then I got an MFA at American University, which I loved—the faculty was great, and I loved being around other writers and having the time and the space to focus on my writing. After I finished the program, I got started on *The Dogs of Babel*. I feel really lucky that I've reached a point where I can write full time, since it's what I've always wanted to do.

## MARISHA PESSL

I haven't always been a writer and I suppose I tiptoed around the idea of writing full time, because it's so isolating. I worked as an actress while in university, and I enjoyed the collaborative aspects of other arts—working on a play or film—which being a novelist is not about. I began writing in my spare time, though, when I was very young, starting when I was in fifth grade. I always had a problem with a short story—whenever I wrote a short story, it ballooned into a novel, so under my belt I have two failed novels that I wrote in college.

I began *Special Topics* when I graduated from college in 2000 and took a financial consulting job at Pricewaterhouse-Coopers, sitting in my cubicle, which everyone at work called a "veal-fattening pen." Sitting like that, I realized I had to get myself out of there, and that was when I first conceptualized Blue and Gareth, the two main characters. The book took me three years to write, and I wrote probably two-thirds of it while I was at PwC. I had no publishing contacts whatsoever, so when I had a relatively polished third draft of the novel, I found a site on the Internet called everyonewhosanyone.com, which lists some three thousand literary-agent e-mail addresses. I resolved to work my way through the list until someone said yes and took me on as a client. Some of my favorite writers, I found out who their agents were, and those were my top choices. Fortunately, I approached ten agents and three offered me representation.

## JOANNA SCOTT

Long ago, I thought I might be a poet. Then I changed my mind, and I started to work on stories—through college, through graduate school. I worked hard, but I felt dissatisfied with the work I was doing. Finally I began a story with the line, "I will tell you how it was." And that became the first line of my first novel. Somehow that insistence that I was just going to tell, no matter what, made the imaginative possibilities of fiction suddenly available to me. But that meant that before I knew it, I was a novelist.

## JHUMPA LAHIRI

My upbringing was essentially being raised by parents who came from one part of the world and who were learning to live in another part of the world. I have two influences all the time. I spoke two languages on a daily basis, I ate two kinds of food, I knew two parts of the world, in a way. I think one of the things that drew me to writing was the opportunity to create my own world. I felt somehow inadequate in both my Indian side and my American side. I always felt I was coming up short somehow, because I was not fully one thing. In writing, I felt I didn't have to answer to anyone's expectations other than my own.

## DAN CHAON

I grew up in a family where no one read books, and I grew up feeling like an oddball in that respect. I feel like I'm around more people now than ever before who love books.

I don't really know why I was so drawn to books. But I remember from an early age wanting to pretend to read books, being fascinated by books, getting books from school and bringing them home, getting books from the library and the bookmobile. I can't quite explain it in any analytical terms. It seemed to be one of those mysterious things like falling in love at first sight. Maybe there's something in my nature that made me attracted to books. I loved the *Poky Little Puppy*, that was a Golden Book. All those Golden Books I remember having great affection for. And then I found a book at a garage sale when I was about five, called *The Violet Fairy Book*, which had all kinds of fairytales from all over the world, and I was very drawn to them.

## ANTHONY DOERR

I guess you could say I've been writing all my life. When I was nine, I was writing stories, but you never think you're going to become a writer. I always told my dad I'd play professional football. You don't say, "I'm going to be a writer when I grow up." At least I didn't. I guess whatever maturity is there may be there because I've been keeping a journal forever. In high school, my friends would make fun of me—"you're doing your man diary again." So I was always trying to translate experience into words. But I didn't start writing seriously until I was twenty-two, writing at night after work. It wasn't until I was twenty-six or twenty-five when I started sending work out to magazines. I feel like it has gone very fast for me, but I feel like it wasn't instantaneous at all. I was getting a lot of rejections. I just got very lucky and it happened quickly for me. I don't feel like I'm a prodigy or something.

## DOREEN BAINGANA

When I left Uganda in 1989 and moved to Italy, I wrote back letters describing everything, because everything was different

—the water tasted different—and it was all new and exciting to me. I would get lost in these letters I was writing. And then when I came to the United States a year later, I used to go to poetry readings and write poetry, and I was taking writing classes at the Writer's Center in Washington, DC, when I became serious about writing.

It's hard to say what I would have done had I stayed in Uganda. I studied law in Uganda, and if I stayed I would have pursued that, and maybe would have had five or six kids by now. And also the process of moving makes you reflect on a lot of things and work through issues that I put in my writing that I wouldn't have had I not moved. But, back in Uganda, there are women writers whom I know who are very good and are pursuing it. And there's a great Uganda women's organization called Femrite, so perhaps I would have been a writer, but perhaps my subject matter would have been different. There are more resources for me here, but people in Uganda are writing with the few resources that they have.


## JOAN SILBER

I always wanted to write. I've been writing since I was in second grade. It never occurred to me. I always wanted to be a writer. The decision to be a writer was made early on.


## TOBIAS WOLFF

The novel *Old School* had been brewing in me for quite a while. I did have a few years in a school somewhat like the one I describe, though different in important ways—this is not a memoir. But it certainly arises to a significant degree from the recollected anxieties, tensions, confusions that I felt as a scholarship boy from the West in an Eastern boarding school whose tone was set by Eastern traditions and mores and a consciousness of class that was new and very disorienting for me.

And I had been trying to understand the roots of my vocation as a writer. I could trace at least part of that vocation to those anxieties and difficulties, because it seemed to me then that becoming a writer was a way of resolving them, that writers formed a class of their own and were thus exempted from the fray. Of course this turned out not to be true—the literary world is as hierarchical and status-obsessed as any other.

## MICHAEL CUNNINGHAM

It took years for me to think of myself as a writer. I wrote for quite some time in secret because I felt like it would be presumptuous and pretentious of me to say that I was a writer. I was just hacking around at it. But gradually, over time, I began to realize that this is what a writer is, someone who sits down every day and tries to write. There is nothing especially magic about it. There was no transformation about to take place. And I began to own up to it. Which was difficult. Because of course, when we start saying to the world or to anyone who will listen, "I'm a writer, and here's what I've written; it's the best I could possibly do," we set ourselves up for rejections of the most withering kind. I've come to believe that a novelist is more than anything else someone who refuses to stop writing and who can stand the disappointment.

As to trying to live while writing, it's just about the hardest part of the whole enterprise. Questions of inspiration pale beside the simple need to pay the rent while writing, which is in itself a full-time occupation. I tended bar, because I could write in the mornings and work at night. And just about the time I was becoming a rather seedy and elderly bartender, the writing started to pay. I am profoundly grateful.

## JOHN DALTON

I wrote an essay called "Done Yet?" about spending eight years writing a novel. For a lot of the eight years I worked on *Heaven Lake,* I had a lot of shame about being an unpublished writer. I think that's a waste of time and angst. If you're a writer and you're working hard every day, you're really doing your best to turn out the very best prose you can, then you're already a writer.

## RICHARD FORD

It probably helped that I didn't know that I was dyslexic when I was young, and I simply thought I was slow as a reader. But being slow made me pore over sentences and be receptive to those qualities in sentences that were not just the cognitive aspect of sentences but were in fact the "poetical" aspects of language—how many syllables a word had, whether it had a long E sound or short I sound, all of those sensuous qualities of language, how it looked on the page. And it seems to me that those qualities in language are as likely to carry weight and hold meaning and give pleasure as the purely cognitive, though of course we can't fundamen-

tally separate those things, although the information age does
its best. The poet Richard Hugo wrote once in an essay that
when language is thought of just as a mode of communica-
tion, it is dying.

I write because I read. And because I read stories when I
was at an impressionable age, when I was in my late teens,
that made an impact on me that was so thorough and so
complex, and it seemed in a way to complete something that
was incomplete about life, that I think I figured out that I
would like to write stories that had effects like that for other
people.

## ALISON SMITH

I didn't know that for a long time. In fact, when I was eighteen, I had the good fortune of meeting and getting to know
Ursula Le Guin. I started college at the University of
Rochester, and they had a winter conference each year, and
that year Ursula Le Guin was the big writer. Every guest was
assigned a student guide. In order to get assigned to a guest,
you had to write an essay about why you should be chosen.
I was so excited. I really wanted to host Ursula Le Guin, so I
wrote an essay. It turned out I was the only person who
applied . . . which is certainly no reflection on Ursula Le
Guin, but it was probably a reflection on the student body.

They gave me a car, sent me to the train station, and I spent
ten days shepherding her around to different events, and in
between she had nothing to do but be entertained by me or
go to her room. So she spent a lot of time with me. One of
the things she said to me was, "Every time I give a talk or
reading, some fool comes up to me and says, 'I want to be a

writer. How do you become a writer?'" She said, "I have no idea how you become a writer. All I know is you write." She said, "I will be interested when someone comes up to me and says, 'I want to write.'"

So I don't know if I'm a writer. But I write.

# 16

# Words of Wisdom

## *What Writers Wish*
## *Someone Had Told Them*

Alison Smith's anecdote about Ursula Le Guin, which ends the previous chapter, probably reflects a sentiment many writers share. How often they are asked: "How do I become a writer?" Well, they think, you might start by writing.

In this chapter, writers answer this question—less simplistically, more specifically, more patiently, but really it's the same answer. ("Read and write and read and write and read and write," Edward P. Jones implores. "Read everything, write all the time," Alice McDermott says.) It isn't any more complex than that.

But then again, it is. They know. Even the most successful writer has had moments of doubt (if not weeks and months of it), and perhaps it is this part of them that has prompted them to give the time and thought about what to say to the tremulous person who comes up and asks them the obvious: "How do you do it? How do I do it?"

In the end, there's only one way to do it. Joyce Carol Oates says it best when she quotes the American artist Chuck

Close: "Amateurs look for inspiration; the rest of us just get up and go to work."

## RICHARD BAUSCH

Nothing is ever wasted. I thought I was writing a novel and it ended up being eight hundred pages of crap around one thing that was real and alive, and unfortunately all of the crap was necessary to arrive at that. If you do this, every single time you do it, you learn stuff. That's why there's only one question to ask yourself every day: "Did you write today?" If the answer's yes, it's the only question you have to ask.

I don't teach writing. I teach patience. Toughness. Stubbornness. The willingness to fail. I teach the life. The odd thing is most of the things that stop an inexperienced writer are so far from the truth as to be nearly beside the point. When you feel global doubt about your talent, that *is* your talent. People who have no talent don't have any doubt. And it's figuring that out and learning how to put all that stuff behind you and just do the work. Just go in and shake the black cue ball and see what surfaces.

## EDWARD P. JONES

Read and write and read and write and read and write, on and on and on. That's essentially it. I mean, if you want to be a golfer, you need land, you need equipment and everything. But if you want to be a writer, you can walk along the street and find a pencil on the ground, and you can peek into a dumpster and find all the paper you need. And libraries are free, so there you are.

## ALICE McDERMOTT

Read everything, write all the time. And if you can do anything else that gives you equal pleasure and allows you to sleep soundly at night, do that instead. The writing life is an odd one, to say the least.

My own "sentimental favorite" is always the novel I haven't yet written—I suppose that's the one I consider my "masterpiece," as well. As Faulkner said, you always write the next novel in order to get at what you failed to get at in the last one. As soon as I write a "masterpiece," I'll retire to the beach in complete self-satisfaction. Seriously, I never look back at finished work, I'm too worried about what's yet to be finished.

## MARISHA PESSL

Writing is not unlike being a plumber. Every day you have a job to do—tell a story. Some days, the work's going to be easy; other days, grueling—when no matter what method you try, the drain (in the kitchen sink perhaps) just refuses to unclog. But if you keep working at it, day after day, you eventually will unclog it. So that's what writing is. You get up every morning. You unclog a few drains.

## MARY KAY ZURAVLEFF

I was at a writers' colony when I was beating the manuscript for *The Bowl Is Already Broken* into submission, and I met Josephine Humphreys, who has many novels under her belt. I asked her for some inspiration, and she said, "The first two are the easy ones. After that, you worry about repeating yourself."

Maybe I've learned to write all the way to the end because

I'm capable of spending a month getting a spring day just right on the page. When I finally found how that scene fit in, the season invariably had changed.

## FRANCES ITANI

Put in the groundwork, write your way through all of the problems, don't sit around thinking about them. You actually have to write your way through them. And don't ever give up. Perhaps the most important, the one I follow myself, is: Follow your instincts.

## MICHAEL CUNNINGHAM

What I want for my students more than anything is to help them write the fiction only *they* can write, fiction that doesn't quite resemble anything we've seen before. And I try to remind them that what they're doing is important, that I love them and others love them for wanting to do it. And that it's better to try too much than to try too little. I'm a big fan of the ambitious failure. And I try to urge them to overreach, to go too far, then look at what they've got and begin to shape it.

## ELIZABETH GRAVER

I did study writing in college, at Wesleyan University, and I was lucky enough to work with the writer Annie Dillard. Annie asked us to memorize poems; I still remember the ones I memorized in her class. She steeped us in language, and she had no tolerance for sentimentality. She was forthright and brilliant and took her students utterly seriously, even as she was quite hilarious herself. In addition to giving me feedback, writing classes also gave me something very simple: deadlines. I think that when you're starting out, it's sometimes hard to keep producing, and even harder to revise and revise and revise. The workshops I took in college gave me a structure, as well as a little community of readers, and that was helpful. I think I would have fumbled along and made my own way without it, but it would have taken longer. I also took many literature courses, and those—along with the reading I did on my own—were as important to my development as a writer as any teacher I've had.


GISH JEN

I went to an MFA program. I went to Iowa. For me it was a wonderful experience. To begin with, it was two years of support. And it was a chance to learn not only from one's own mistakes but also from the mistakes of others. So you're spared having to make all the mistakes yourself, which is very time-consuming. I don't know that MFA programs are for everyone, and I think a lot depends on who's teaching. But for me, it was a great experience.


JHUMPA LAHIRI

Discouragement and hitting walls and feeling lost—it's just part of the process. You can't really create without confronting those things. Trying to meet with those challenges and work through them is what it's all about. It's sort of like solving a puzzle. It's not meant to be easy.

I think MFA programs can be helpful. I think one shouldn't have unreasonable expectations, but I think they're helpful in that they force you to write—which is the essential thing, after all—and they can give you very helpful feedback and make you look at your work in a more objective way, which I think is necessary for a writer. I think they're valuable in the sense that they force you to write on a regular basis and they open your eyes, in a way.

But I don't think people should assume that an MFA program will necessarily lead to publication, or overnight literary success, or anything like that. I'm sure that some people experience that, but for the majority of people, it's a way to make writing a priority in your life, and you sort of take it from there. It's not so much what you learn in your time in the program but how it teaches you the work for the rest of your life.

## ANTHONY DOERR

I did go to an MFA program, at Bowling Green State University in Ohio. It was a small program—they only take five fiction writers a year, and they fund all of us—you don't go into debt to get an MFA. It's not like getting an MBA—you're not going to buy yourself out. For me it was perfect, because it wasn't a very competitive environment, and it was a studio program. They basically send you off and say, bring us some work and we'll help you improve it. It really rewarded self-discipline. So I guess my answer is way too complicated to say that I believe in them in general. When they work well, it's two years for someone to really work on their writing. But the problems with them are pretty obvious—people go in thinking they're going to meet an agent and get published instead of taking that time to write. And it is occasionally a refuge for people who don't know what else to do with their lives. Every aspiring writer should evaluate that decision for him- or herself.

## HANNAH TINTI

I think there are two things that helped me. One was I went to a writers' colony and got a chunk of time to get away and write and meet other writers. I went to Hedgebrook, off the coast of Seattle. I think of my life pre-Hedgebrook and post-Hedgebrook. I'd suggest people investigate writers' colonies.

And the second thing about the publishing side of things is to somehow get involved in the literary community—volunteer at a literary magazine—to learn the other side of what it's like to have work coming into you, and learn the process and what's out there: what other people are writing. Or working at a bookstore. I got a job interning at the *Boston Review*, and I read all the slush. It taught me how to write a story; it showed me what not to do and how to present my own work.

## CLAIRE TRISTRAM

You just need to write. The best way to learn how to write is to read, and then do it. Very simply, successful writing is when you are listening to yourself very deeply and you have something to say. It's a very solitary, quiet, meditative process and you have to be patient enough to have that happen on the page. And trust that you have something to say.

## JOHN DALTON

Don't waste time feeling ashamed for being an unpublished writer. Each time you sit alone in a room and give your most honest and complete effort, you've earned the title of *writer*, particularly on those days when you struggle the hardest, when you spend all afternoon and evening refining an idea or the precise phrasing of a few descriptions, when you're pushing yourself beyond your own abilities. These hard-fought and seemingly inconsequential victories accumulate over time and make all the difference.

I think there is a ponderousness and pretentiousness in the writing community, but you shouldn't be deterred by that. There's also a great deal of generosity. I've met so many fiction writers, poets, and artists who are very kind and generous people. I think it's perfectly okay to accept an open hand when it's offered out of generosity and integrity. That's a fine thing to do. And MFA programs and artists' colonies—I just got back from MacDowell—they're wonderful because they allow you to have these wonderful friendships in your life that are important creatively and personally.

## DAN CHAON

The best advice I can give to anybody is that it is for most people a very long process, and you can't be too tied to results, because you can't control most of what happens to you. The only thing you can control is the effort and quality that goes into your own work. Sometimes you're lucky. I know people who have been very lucky with their work, and I know people who have been very unlucky, and it doesn't seem to have much to do with quality.

If it's important to you and you can capture something vividly, it's worth doing. And there's no way to gauge whether other people will care or not. But I suspect that if you've done something that pleases you and moves you, there are other people out there who will also be interested.

## ALISON SMITH

I think the hardest part about being a writer is facing yourself. It's just like everybody else: It's managing your coworkers, except that your coworkers are all in your head. You end up developing a complicated and complex relationship with yourself, because you are alone most of the time and your tools are memory and imagination. The hardest part and the best part about being a writer is creating that relationship with yourself—your structure, your guidelines, how you treat yourself. Right inside your head are your entire office politics, your deadlines, your coworkers. How do you manage that world in your head?

## JOAN SILBER

Sometimes what people are asking is, "What do I do in the face of defeat?" And I do have two answers to that. One is to cultivate equanimity. And the other is to realize that there is more to life than writing.

## JOYCE CAROL OATES

Most writers much of the time experience difficulty with writing first drafts. Everyone will say this. Beginning writers may become overly discouraged by the difficulties that more experienced writers expect. We are often "blocked" for periods of time, but if we work and keep writing and above all keep thinking about the project, almost always a pathway will open to us. Sometimes I feel as if I were on the outside of a hedge, a thicket, and there seems to be no way in, and I keep circling this thicket and finally I will find a way in. It might be very small, but it's a way in—a phrase or a sentence or an image or a character speaking to me—and this will be the beginning of what will not be in fact an easy experience. I will close with a quote from an artist, Chuck Close: "Amateurs look for inspiration; the rest of us just get up and go to work."

# Authors' Biographies

**Martin Amis**'s best sellers include the novels *House of Meetings, London Fields,* and *The Information,* as well his memoir, *Experience.* His work includes eleven novels, six books of non-fiction, two short-story collections, and hundreds of reviews and essays. He has received the Somerset Maugham Award for best first novel and the James Tait Black Memorial Prize for biography. His work is routinely shortlisted for other awards, including the Man Booker Prize. He lives in London.

Amis's advice on writing a novel: "Get to the end, and then worry. But get to the end."

**Marie Arana** is the editor of the *Washington Post Book World.* Born in Peru of a Peruvian father and an American mother, she is the author most recently of a novel, *Cellophane.* Her memoir, *American Chica,* was a finalist for the PEN-Memoir Award and the National Book Award, and she has also edited a collection of columns, *The Writing Life: Writers on How They Think and Work.* Arana lives in Washington, DC, and Lima, Peru.

**Paul Auster** is the best-selling author of thirteen novels (including *The Brooklyn Follies, Oracle Night,* and *The New York Trilogy*) and four screenplays (including *Smoke* and *Blue in the Face,* which he co-directed with Wayne Wang). In 2006, Auster was inducted into the American Academy of Arts and Letters. He also won Spain's most prestigious prize for literature—the Premio Principe de Asturias de las Letras. Among his other awards are the Commandeur de l'Ordre des Arts et des Lettres and the Prix Médicis for the best foreign novel published in France. His work has been translated into thirty-five languages.

**Doreen Baingana** is a Ugandan writer and author of *Tropical Fish: Stories Out of Entebbe.* The book won the Associated Writers and Writing Programs (AWP) Award in Short Fiction and the Commonwealth Writers' Prize for First Book, Africa Region, and was a finalist for the Hurston-Wright Prize for Debut Fiction. She was a two-time finalist for the Caine Prize for African Writing. Her fiction and essays have been published in such journals as *Glimmer Train, Chelsea* and *The Guardian.* Baingana lives in the United States.

Baingana writes: "I try to read poetry instead of the newspaper with my breakfast every day. Disasters can wait. I'd rather feed my early morning mind on beautiful words reaching for the essence of experience."

**Russell Banks** is the author of fifteen works of fiction, including the novels *Continental Drift, Cloudsplitter,* and *The Darling,* and several short-story collections. Two of his novels, *The Sweet Hereafter* and *Affliction,* have been made into award-winning motion pictures. His work has received numerous awards and has been widely translated and anthologized. Banks is a member of the American Academy of Arts and Letters and is president of the North American Network of Cities of Asylum. He lives in upstate New York with his wife, the poet Chase Twichell.

"The short motto I've kept over my desk for forty years now is just this: Remember Death."

**Richard Bausch** is the author of ten novels and seven story collections, including *Hello to the Cannibals, The Stories of Richard Bausch*, and, most recently, *Thanksgiving Night*. He has been awarded the PEN/Malamud Award for Short Fiction and his work has appeared in *The Atlantic Monthly, The New Yorker*, and elsewhere. Other honors include a Guggenheim Fellowship, a Lila Wallace–*Reader's Digest* Writer's Award, and the Award of the American Academy of Arts and Letters. Editor of *The Norton Anthology of Short Fiction*, he currently serves as the Moss Chair of Excellence in the Writing Program at the University of Memphis.

"Writing well, striving for exact expression, is an act of mental health, every time it happens. It is an exercise of all the human virtues—generosity, hope, belief in others, loyalty, forgiveness, grace, patience and, yes, love."

**Charles Baxter** is the author of four novels, including *Saul and Patsy* and *The Feast of Love*, a finalist for the National Book Award, and four books of short stories, most recently, *Believers*. He has published essays on fiction collected in *Burning Down the House* and, in 2007, *Beyond Plot,* and has edited or coedited three books of essays. Born in Minneapolis in 1947, he lived for many years in Ann Arbor, Michigan, where he taught at the University of Michigan. Now living in Minneapolis, he is the Edelstein-Keller Professor of Creative Writing at the University of Minnesota.

"I can't do better than Henry James: 'We work in the dark; we do what we can . . . the rest is the madness of art.' "

**A. S. Byatt** is the author of several novels, books of short stories and criticism. Her works have been translated into at least twenty-eight languages. *Possession* won the Man Booker Prize and the *Irish Times* Aer Lingus Prize in 1990. Her most recent novel is *A Whistling Woman* (2002), the final book in a quartet, which also includes *The Virgin in the Garden, Still Life*, and *Babel Tower*. This was followed by *Little Black Book of Stories* (2003).

"My favorite quotation is Wallace Stevens. 'To find/not to impose . . . It is possible, possible, possible. It must be/ Possible.' "

**Dan Chaon**'s books include the novel *You Remind Me of Me* and the short-story collection *Among the Missing*, which was a finalist for the National Book Award. Chaon's stories have appeared in many journals and anthologies including *Best American Short Stories*, *The O. Henry Prize Stories*, and *The Pushcart Prize Anthology*. He was, most recently, the recipient of the 2006 Academy Award in Literature from the American Academy of Arts and Letters.

"Don't listen to anyone who has snazzy, pithy advice about the writing process."

**Michael Cunningham** is the author of four novels, including *The Hours*, which won a Pulitzer Prize and the PEN/Faulkner award in 1999. His most recent novel is *Specimen Days*. He is the recipient of a Whiting Writers' Award, a Guggenheim Fellowship, a National Endowment for the Arts Fellowship, and a Michener Fellowship from the University of Iowa. He lives in New York City.

**John Dalton** is the author of the novel *Heaven Lake*, published by Scribner, and winner of the 2004 Barnes and Noble Discover Award and the Sue Kaufman Prize for First Fiction from the American Academy of Arts and Letters. He teaches in the writing program at the University of Missouri–St. Louis.

"Pay close attention to the best, truest, most articulate and elegant writing in your manuscript. These five-star passages will show you how to remedy the other passages that are problematic or merely mediocre."

**E. L. Doctorow's** work includes the novels *Ragtime, World's Fair*, and, most recently, *The March*, which won him the 2006 PEN/Faulkner Award for Fiction. His other honors include the National Book Award, two National Book Critics Circle awards, the 1990 PEN/Faulkner Award, the Edith Wharton Citation for Fiction, the William Dean Howells Medal of the American Academy of Arts and Letters, and the presidentially conferred National Medal for the Humanities (1998). He lives and works in New York.

**Anthony Doerr** is the author of a short-story collection, *The Shell Collector*; a novel, *About Grace*; and a memoir, *Four Seasons in Rome: On Twins, Insomnia, and the Biggest Funeral in the History of the World*. His work has won the New York Public Library's Young Lions Award, the Barnes and Noble Discover Prize, two O. Henry Prizes, two Ohioana Book Awards, and the Rome Prize from the American Academy of

Arts and Letters. He also writes the "On Science" column for the *Boston Globe.*

"The wonderful, fabulous thing about writing is that in any library—for free!—is the work of so many masters, so many sentence-makers. Even if they're dead, their books are still there, bristling with life, waiting to show you what they do with adjectives, how they employ verbs."

**Stuart Dybek** is the author of three books of fiction, including *I Sailed With Magellan* and *The Coast of Chicago,* which was a One Book, One Chicago selection. Dybek has also published two collections of poetry. Among his numerous awards are a PEN/Malamud Award for Short Fiction, a Lannan Literary Award, a Whiting Writers' Award, an award from the American Academy of Arts and Letters, several O. Henry Prizes, and fellowships from the National Endowment for the Arts and the Guggenheim Foundation. He is Distinguished Writer in Residence at Northwestern University and a member of the permanent faculty for Western Michigan University's Prague Summer Program.

"In one of James Farrell's novels, a neighborhood tough asks a young Danny O'Neal—Farrell's stand-in for a writer—'what makes good writing,' to which O'Neal answers, 'Life on the page.' That's long been the standard for me."

**Richard Ford** is the author of three collections of short fiction and six novels, including *Independence Day,* which won the 1996 Pulitzer Prize and the PEN/Faulkner Award for Fiction. His other work includes the short-story collection *Rock Springs,* and, most recently, the novel *The Lay of the Land.* Ford has also been awarded the PEN/Malamud Award for Short Fiction. He lives in Maine and New Orleans.

**Tod Goldberg** is the author of three books of fiction, including the novel *Living Dead Girl*, a finalist for the *Los Angeles Times* Book Prize, and, most recently, the short-story collection *Simplify*. His nonfiction appears regularly in the *Los Angeles Times, Las Vegas CityLife*, and other publications. He lives in La Quinta, California, with his wife, Wendy, and teaches creative writing at the UCLA Extension Writers' Program.

"Whenever I sit down to write, I'm aiming for the green light at the end of the dock."

**Elizabeth Graver** is the author of three novels: *Awake, The Honey Thief*, and *Unravelling*. Her short-story collection, *Have You Seen Me?*, was awarded the 1991 Drue Heinz Literature Prize. Her stories and essays have been anthologized in *Best American Short Stories; The O. Henry Prize Stories; Best American Essays;* and *The Pushcart Prize Anthology.* The recipient of fellowships from the National Endowment for the Arts and the Guggenheim Foundation, she teaches at Boston College and is the mother of two young daughters.

"You absolutely don't need to know where you're going, but it helps to be a hardy, determined, passionate traveller."

*The Great Fire*, **Shirley Hazzard**'s first published work of fiction in more than twenty years, won the National Book Award in 2003. Born in Australia, she has written three other novels, including *The Bay of Noon* (1971) and *The Transit of Venus* (1981), which won the National Book Critics Circle Award. She is also the author of two collections of short stories and several works of nonfiction, including a memoir on Graham Greene, *Greene on Capri*. She lives in New York and travels frequently to Italy.

**Pam Houston** is the author of two collections of linked short stories, *Cowboys Are My Weakness*, which was the winner of the 1993 Western States Book Award, and *Waltzing the Cat*, which won the WILLA Award for Contemporary Fiction. Her stories have been selected for volumes of *Best American Short Stories*, *The O. Henry Prize Stories*, *The Pushcart Prize Anthology*, and *Best American Short Stories of the Century*. Her first novel, *Sight Hound,* was a finalist for the Colorado Book Award. She is the director of Creative Writing at UC–Davis and divides her time between Colorado and California.

"Here is something I believe in like religion: No matter how awful the prospect of sitting down at my desk and writing might feel, I know that there will come a day, in the not too distant future, where it will feel even worse not to."

**Maureen Howard** is the author of seven novels, including *Grace Abounding, Expensive Habits*, and *Natural History*, all of which were nominated for the PEN/Faulkner Award. She has taught at a number of American universities, including Columbia, Princeton, Amherst, and Yale, and was recently awarded the Academy Award in Literature by the American Academy of Arts and Letters. She lives in New York City. Her most recent novel is *The Silver Screen*.

"Bumpersticker above my desk: Honk if you love Borges."

**Frances Itani**, a Member of the Order of Canada, grew up in the Province of Quebec and now lives in Ottawa. She has written eleven books, including the international best seller *Deafening*, which has been translated into seventeen languages; won a Commonwealth Writers' Prize; and was short-listed for both the International IMPAC Dublin and the

William Saroyan International Literary Awards. She has written for Canadian Broadcasting Corporation (CBC) radio and reviews for *The Washington Post*. Her new novel is called *Remembering the Bones*.

"Where do you start work each day on your manuscript? I was once given this great advice:'You go where it grabs you the most.' "

**Gish Jen** has been published in *The New Yorker, The Atlantic Monthly, The New Republic, The Los Angeles Times,* and *The New York Times,* as well as in numerous textbooks and anthologies, including *The Best American Short Stories of the Century,* edited by John Updike. Her books, including *Who's Irish?, Typical American,* and, most recently, *The Love Wife,* have been supported by a number of organizations, such as the Lannan Foundation, the Guggenheim Foundation, the Radcliffe Institute for Advanced Study, the Fulbright Program, and the National Endowment for the Arts. She currently holds a Mildred and Harold Strauss "Living Award" from the American Academy of Arts and Letters.

"I do often think of something Sister Wendy Beckett said, namely:'Use everything.' "

**Edward P. Jones**'s novel, *The Known World,* won the Pulitzer Prize for Fiction, the National Book Critics Circle Award, the International IMPAC Dublin Literary Award, and the Lannan Literary Award. He also received a MacArthur Fellowship in 2004. His first collection of short stories, *Lost in the City,* won the Hemingway/PEN Award and was shortlisted for the National Book Award. Most recently, he has published *All Aunt Hagar's Children: Stories.* He lives in Washington, DC.

**Jhumpa Lahiri**'s debut collection of stories, *Interpreter of Maladies*, won the 2000 Pulitzer Prize for Fiction, the Hemingway/PEN Award, the *New Yorker* Debut of the Year Award, and an Addison Metcalf Award from the American Academy of Arts and Letters. Translated into thirty-three languages, it was a best seller in the United States and abroad. Lahiri was awarded a Guggenheim Fellowship in 2002 and a National Endowment for the Arts grant in 2006. Her most recent book is *The Namesake*, her first novel. Born in 1967 in London and raised in Rhode Island, she lives in New York with her husband and two children.

"I recently read Orhan Pamuk's Nobel lecture and was moved by his succinct explanation of what a writer does: 'He must have the artistry to tell his own stories as if they were other people's stories, and to tell other people's stories as if they were his own.' "

**Andrea Levy**'s most recent novel, *Small Island*, won the 2004 Orange Prize for Fiction, the Whitbread Novel Award, the Whitbread Book of the Year Award, and the Commonwealth Writers' Prize. It also won the Best of the Best Award, chosen in 2005 from the first ten years of Orange Prize winners. She has written three other novels, including *Fruit of the Lemon*, and her short stories and reviews have been aired on the BBC and published in *The Guardian* and elsewhere. She lives in London.

**Margot Livesey** was born and grew up on the edge of the Scottish Highlands. She is the author of a collection of stories and five novels, most recently *Eva Moves the Furniture* and *Banishing Verona*. She is the recipient of grants from the Guggenheim Foundation and the National Endowment for the Arts and is currently a writer in residence at Emerson College in Boston. Her new novel, *Child's Play*, is coming out from HarperCollins in summer 2008.

"I always come back to W. H. Auden's simple and profound advice to a young writer: 'Write about what interests you.' "

**Alice McDermott's** *Charming Billy* won the National Book Award in 1998. She is the author of five other novels, including *At Weddings and Wakes*, a *New York Times* best seller, and *After This,* published in 2006. She lives with her family near Washington, DC.

"Faulkner's Nobel Prize acceptance speech has been so much quoted, it's nearly become cliché, but when I first came upon it, at nineteen, it inspired, especially this part: 'He'—the young writer—'must teach himself that the basest of all things is to be afraid, and, teaching himself that, forget it forever, leaving no room in his workshop for anything but the old verities and truths of the human heart . . .' "

**John McNally** is the author of two novels, *America's Report Card* and *The Book of Ralph*. His previous collection, *Troublemakers*, won the John Simmons Short Fiction Award (2000) and was a *Book Sense 76* selection. McNally's fiction has appeared in more than forty journals and magazines, and he frequently reviews books for *The Washington Post* and other newspapers. He has edited five anthologies, most recently *When I Was a Loser* (Free Press, 2007). A native of Chicago's southwest side, he is the Ollen R. Nalley Associate Professor of English at Wake Forest University. He and his wife, Amy, live in Winston-Salem, North Carolina.

"This may be basic to the point of sounding stupid, but if you want to write, you need to read. You need to learn why one book is great and why another one is crappy, and you need to understand why *it's not all subjective!*"

**Walter Mosley** is the author of more than thirty critically acclaimed books and his work has been translated into twenty-one languages. His popular mysteries featuring Easy Rawlins began in 1990 with *Devil in a Blue Dress*; his most recent Rawlins novel, *Blonde Faith*, was published in 2007. He has published three books of literary fiction, including *The Man in the Basement*, and three books of nonfiction, most recently one about writing: *This Year You Write Your Novel*. His numerous awards include the Anisfield-Wolf Book Award, which honors work that increases understanding of race in America.

**Thisbe Nissen** is the author of two novels, *Osprey Island* and *The Good People of New York*, and a story collection, *Out of the Girls' Room and into the Night*. She also coauthored and co-illustrated *The Ex-Boyfriend Cookbook*. A graduate of Oberlin College and the Iowa Writers' Workshop, she is currently the Fanny Hurst Writer in Residence at Brandeis University.

Her favorite line about writing is from Isaac Babel, who said: "Your language becomes clear and strong not when you can no longer add, but when you can no longer take away."

**Joyce Carol Oates** is a recipient of the National Book Award and the PEN/Malamud Award for Short Fiction. Her many books of fiction and nonfiction include national best sellers *We Were the Mulvaneys, Blonde,* and *The Falls*, which won the 2005 Prix Femina. She is the Roger S. Berlind Distinguished Professor in the Humanities at Princeton University, and, since 1978, she has been a member of the American Academy of Arts and Letters. In 2003, she received the Commonwealth Award for Distinguished Service in Literature and the Kenyon Review Award for Literary Achievement.

"No single thought keeps me going, as no single thought would stop me. But I quite admire Emily Dickinson's terse verse: 'Success is counted sweetest/By those who ne'er succeed.'"

**Carolyn Parkhurst** is the author of *Lost and Found* and the *New York Times* best-selling novel *The Dogs of Babel*, which was a Today Show Book Club pick and a *New York Times* Notable Book and has been translated into twenty languages. She lives in Washington, DC, with her husband and their two children.

"Pay attention to how you feel when you're writing," she says. "If you hit on something that feels uncomfortable or a little bit scary, don't avoid it; some of the most honest work comes from writing about things we're not sure we should be writing about."

**Tim Parks** has written eleven novels, including *Europa, Judge Savage*, and, most recently, *Cleaver*, as well as three nonfiction accounts of life in northern Italy, two collections of essays, and *Medici Money*, a history of the Medici bank in fifteenth-century Florence. His many translations from the Italian include works by Alberto Moravia and Italo Calvino. He lectures on literary translation in Milan and has published a book that analyzes Italian translations of English modernists. Born in Manchester in 1954, he grew up in London and studied at Cambridge and Harvard. In 1981, he moved to Italy, where he has lived ever since.

About writing, he says: "It's a long haul. Remember to enjoy it."

**Marisha Pessl** is the author of the *New York Times* best seller *Special Topics in Calamity Physics*. It has been translated into eighteen languages and was named one of the ten Best Books of 2006 by *The New York Times*. She grew up in Asheville, North Carolina, and currently lives in New York City.

**Joanna Scott** is the author of seven novels, including *Arrogance,* and two collections of short fiction, most recently *Everybody Loves Somebody*. Her fiction and essays have appeared in *The Paris Review, Harper's, Esquire,* and other journals. Her books have been finalists for the Pulitzer Prize, the PEN/Faulkner Award, and the *Los Angeles Times* Book Prize. Her awards include a MacArthur Fellowship, a Lannan Literary Award, a Guggenheim Fellowship, the Ambassador Book Award from the English-Speaking Union, and the Rosenthal Award from the American Academy of Arts and Letters. She is the Roswell Smith Burrows Professor of English at the University of Rochester.

For her students, Scott once wrote "Unreliable Guidelines for the Art of Fiction"—part spoof, part passion. Number thirteen is: "Insist on the specificity of place and the consequence of action."

**Joan Silber** is the author of *Ideas of Heaven: A Ring of Stories,* a finalist for the National Book Award and the Story Prize. Her four other books of fiction include *Household Words,* winner of a Hemingway/PEN Award, recently reissued by W. W. Norton. Her work has been chosen for the *O. Henry Prize Stories* and *The Pushcart Prize* anthologies and has appeared in

*The New Yorker, Ploughshares,* and *The Paris Review.* Her next novel will be published by Norton in 2008. She lives in New York City and teaches at Sarah Lawrence College.

"I always tell people who want to write: Focus on the work itself," she says. "Conversely, you have to remember the world contains a lot more than writing. Cultivate equanimity, or you'll drive yourself nuts."

**Alison Smith**'s memoir, *Name All the Animals,* was a *New York Times* Notable Book and was named one of the top ten books of 2004 by *People* magazine. Awards include the Barnes and Noble Discover Award, the Judy Grahn Prize, the Fountain Award for Speculative Fiction, a Lambda Literary Award, and the William Sloane Fellowship. Smith's writing has appeared in *Granta, McSweeney's, The London Telegraph, The New York Times, The Believer,* and other publications. She lives in Brooklyn, New York.

"There's a piece of paper with a sentence taped to my monitor," she says. "It's a Seamus Heaney quote, and it reads: 'All I know is a door into the dark.'"

Winner of a special Pulitzer Prize in 1992 for his Holocaust narratives in comics form, *Maus* and *Maus II,* **Art Spiegelman**'s best-selling collection of 9/11 strips, *In the Shadow of No Towers,* was a *New York Times* Notable Book of 2004. Recipient of a Guggenheim Fellowship and creator of Garbage Pail Kids, his work has been published in many periodicals, including *The New Yorker,* where he was a staff artist and writer from 1993 to 2003. With his wife, Françoise Mouly, he edited the influential graphics magazine *RAW* (1980–1991) and more recently *Little Lit,* a series of comics anthologies for kids. They live in New York City with their two children, Nadja and Dash.

**Hannah Tinti** grew up in Salem, Massachusetts. Her work has appeared in various magazines and anthologies, including *Best American Mystery Stories 2003*. Her short-story collection, *Animal Crackers*, has sold in fifteen countries and was recently a runner-up for the Hemingway/PEN Award. Her novel, *Resurrection Men*, is forthcoming from Dial Press. She is the cofounder and editor of *One Story* magazine.

"I'm a recreational potter, and something I try to apply to my writing is this—that you have to make the clay before you make the pot. In other words, just get something, anything, on the page, then go back and create the structure and form."

**Colm Tóibín** is the author of five novels, including *The Master*, which won the International IMPAC Dublin Literary Award, the *Los Angeles Times* Novel of the Year, and the *Prix du Meilleur Livre Etranger* for the best foreign novel published in 2005 in France. Along with *The Master*, his novel *The Blackwater Lightship* was shortlisted for the Man Booker Prize. He has also published several books of nonfiction and, most recently, a collection of stories, *Mothers and Sons*. Born in Enniscorthy in the southeast of Ireland, he lives in Dublin.

**Claire Tristram** is the author of the novel *After*.

"As I'm working on a novel," she writes, "I never ask myself if the writing is 'good,' which seems to invoke in me an impossible Platonic ideal and to make me want to give up. Instead, I always ask myself if the writing is 'good enough,' which somehow frees me to write the best way I can."

**Tobias Wolff**'s books include the memoirs *This Boy's Life* and *In Pharaoh's Army: Memories of the Lost War*; the short novel

*The Barracks Thief*; three collections of stories, including *The Night in Question*; and, most recently, the novel *Old School*. His work is translated widely and has received numerous awards, including the PEN/Faulkner Award for Fiction, the *Los Angeles Times* Book Prize, the PEN/Malamud Award for Short Fiction, the Rea Award for the Short Story, and the Academy Award in Literature from the American Academy of Arts and Letters. He is the Ward W. and Priscilla B. Woods Professor of English at Stanford University.

"The thought that keeps me going?" he says. "This—patience."

**Mary Kay Zuravleff** is the author of *The Frequency of Souls* and *The Bowl Is Already Broken*. She has received the Rosenthal Award from the American Academy of Arts and Letters and the James Jones First Novel Fellowship Award. She lives in Washington, DC, and teaches at George Mason University.

When writing, she aims herself at the last lines of Marie Howe's poem "The Meadow," which suggests that the stories we tell are already dormant within us, and implores the writer to find words "that even now sleep on your tongue, and to know that tangled/among them and terribly new is the sentence that could change your life."

# Acknowledgments

For their work both on and off the page, I would like to thank every author who has appeared in this book—for venturing on to the online interview format, for giving such honest, intelligent answers, and most of all, for their dedication to their work. They are an inspiration. Without them, this book wouldn't exist.

For their support both on and off the page, I would like to thank Amy Cherry, for her perceptive editing and her passion for books (and not just mine); Rolph Blythe, for his willingness to work with me at an early stage and his patient faith in this project; Jim Brady, Tim Ruder, and the entire Live Online team at washington post.com, who have lent their expertise since the very first "Off the Page" interview; Marie Arana, for her steady support throughout the project; and Paul Edwards, for his ideas about "colour," teaching art history backward, as well as many, many other wonderful things.